WILTSHIRE AND SOMERSET WOOLLEN WEAVERS

Wiltshire and Somerset Woollen Weavers

K.H. & E.J. Rogers

THE HOBNOB PRESS

First published in the United Kingdom in 2025

by The Hobnob Press,
8 Lock Warehouse, Severn Road, Gloucester GL1 2GA
www.hobnobpress.co.uk

© K.H. and E.J. Rogers 2025

The Authors hereby assert their moral rights to be identified as the Authors of the Work.

All rights reserved. No part of this publication may be reproduced, stored in a retrieval system, or transmitted in any form or by any means, electronic, mechanical, photocopying, recording or otherwise, without the prior permission of the publisher and copyright holder.

British Library Cataloguing in Publication Data
A catalogue record for this book is available from the British Library

ISBN 978-1-914407-81-9

Typeset in Adobe Garamond Pro, 11/14 pt
Typesetting and origination by John Chandler

CONTENTS

Preface by Ken Rogers
Maps of Trowbridge and West Wiltshire
Introduction   1

Cottage weaving   7
In the Town   7
Places close to the town   10
    The outer parts of the parish   16
        The Studleys   16
    Hilperton Marsh   27
    Nearby villages   29
    Steeple Ashton parish   29
    North Bradley and Southwick   31
    Dilton Marsh   34
What were the weaver's houses like?   35
    Weaving shops within cottages   37
    The Three Storied Weavers' Houses   41
    The town centre   76
        Staverton and over the parish boundary   78
    Other towns   80

Shop Weaving   82
Cassimeres and the Fancy Trade   82
    Opposition to shop weaving   86
    Changes of fortune in the Fancy Trade   90
    The beginning of shop weaving in factories   97
    The revival of the fancy trade   99

Factory weaving: power looms — 107
The introduction of power looms in the area — 107
    The spread of power looms in Trowbridge — 111
    Power looms in other towns — 116
    The last days of handweaving — 120

The organisation of weaving — 126
    Theft of materials — 126
    The prosecution of 1862 — 132
    The resulting correspondence — 134
    Strokes — 141
    The charges against the book keepers — 143
    The correspondents — 145
    Other book keepers — 146

The life of the weavers — 151
    The improvident weaver — 152
    The defence of the weavers — 155
    The prosperous weaver — 158
    Apprentices and journeymen — 162
    The factory weaver and the factory owners — 164
    Truck — 167
    The conservative weaver — 171
    The Radical Weaver — 173

Conclusion — 179

Index — 180

PREFACE

BY KEN ROGERS

When I began to sort the large accumulation of notes during many years' work on the local woollen industry, I was struck by how little had been written about weavers and weaving – how the weavers made a living, even how the looms worked. Miss Mann, the doyenne of textile historians, in her magisterial *The Cloth Industry in the West of England from 1640 to 1880*, has virtually nothing to say on the way in which cottage weaving was able to hold its own against the advance of the power loom for a quarter of a century.

I began to work towards a book which could remedy this, but failing sight halted this. When I recruited my son Edward to help me on the computer, he immediately made himself a master of all aspects of the subject, revised what I had written, and added much material from further research. This book is as much his as mine.

I should point out here that the area covered in this book is that in my *Wiltshire and Somerset Woollen Mills* published in 1976, woollen being a technical term to distinguish our product from the worsted-type products made in west Somerset and Devon.

Ken Rogers
January 2025

Kenneth H Rogers, former Wiltshire County Archivist and leading authority on the history of Trowbridge and the West Country textile industry, died on 26 January 2025, age 94. With his son Edward's help he lived to see this book completed and to know that its publication was imminent.

*Trowbridge street plan c.1860, by J. Howell
(WSA, G15/1/89 PC, reproduced with permission of Wiltshire Council)*

The West Wiltshire clothing district, detail from Andrews and Dury's index map to their map of Wiltshire, 2nd edn. 1810

INTRODUCTION

IN THE THIRTIES and forties, when I was a boy, Trowbridge was still a centre of cloth manufacture, with five firms occupying six factories. Also in the area were one firm at Westbury with two factories, one large and two small firms at Frome, and one firm at Twerton. Now, when we walk through the Shires Shopping Centre in Trowbridge we pass through the lower part of Home Mill, the main part of the factory of Samuel Salter and Co. Its closure in 1982 marked the end of six centuries of cloth manufacture in the town, and indeed in the valley of the Bristol Avon and its tributaries. In this area and in Stroud and its valleys (where one firm is still in business) were made the cloths proudly known as 'West of England' to distinguish them from lower quality and cheaper goods made elsewhere.

Until about 1790 this manufacture was mainly carried out domestically, that is, at the houses either of the employer or of his workpeople. The only exceptions were fulling, which needed the power supplied by a water mill, and scouring and dyeing the wool, which needed running water. From 1790 onwards machinery became available for all processes, leading to the erection of factories driven firstly by water power and then by steam engines. Weaving was, however, the last process to be mechanized. The power loom came into use in this area from 1847, but only gradually replaced handloom weaving.

Weavers like my maternal great-great and great grandparents, George and James Beaven, still at their looms in Studley in the 1870s, were the remnant of a domestic system going back to the Middle Ages.

This book on weavers and weaving is based on the notes I have accumulated over many years[1]. We need to begin with some definitions:

A **clothier** owned the material throughout the processes of manufacture – he bought the wool, and he sold the cloth, or had it sold on his behalf. This might seem obvious, but it was not so everywhere. In Yorkshire, for instance, weavers often wove cloths from their own materials and took them to Piece

---

1 For further detail about the manufacturing processes referred to throughout, see *Woollen Industry Processes*, K H Rogers, Friends of Trowbridge Museum

Halls like the one still standing at Halifax, to sell on to someone to finish. Many clothiers in our area were men of great wealth, as we can see from their houses both of the domestic and factory periods. In domestic times the clothier usually had workshops adjoining his house where some processes were carried on, but not weaving. It was here that the weaver came to collect the yarn for his piece, and to here he brought his piece, often after three or four weeks. Later, of course, handing out was done at the factory.

Cottage Weaving. In this book there is a constant distinction between cottage weaving and shop weaving. Apart from one early venture, shop weaving was not known before 1766. The essential point about cottage weaving is that it was carried out on the weaver's premises. The cottage could range from a one-roomed hovel to a substantial house which included a [work]shop which might contain several looms, worked on by the weaver himself, other members of his family, or other weavers employed by him. Cottage weaving continued until the final end of handloom weaving about 1880.

Shop weaving was done in a [work]shop provided by an employer, often, though not always, the clothier. The practice began on the introduction from 1766 onwards of new types of cloth which were more complicated to weave. Although at times disliked, for different reasons, both by clothiers and weavers, there was a gradual tendency to have some weaving (still handloom) done in shops at the factories.

Warping on pegs prior to use in the loom

Handloom weaving is a complicated process, and one on which we are ill-qualified to comment. The weaver would go to his master's 'wool loft' and collect there the yarn necessary for his cloth. The wool loft was supervised either by the clothier himself or by an employee called a bookkeeper or a wool loft man[2]. The cloth for the warp (the lengthwise threads, commonly called in our area the chain) will have been warped, that is, measured out in length for the cloths required; the picture will make it clear how this was usually done. The west also had its own nomenclature for the weft, the crosswise threads inserted by the shuttle – the abb or the shoot (no doubt pronounced to rhyme with put).

The warp was often strengthened by treating it with a thin glue called size, and then had to be dried hung out in the open air. It then had to be inserted into the loom. These diagrams show typical arrangements of a handloom.

This diagram shows a four treadle handloom. The up and down motion of the treadles is transmitted to the side of the loom by the shafts marked DD, and thence up and over the loom to the harnesses[3], marked AB.

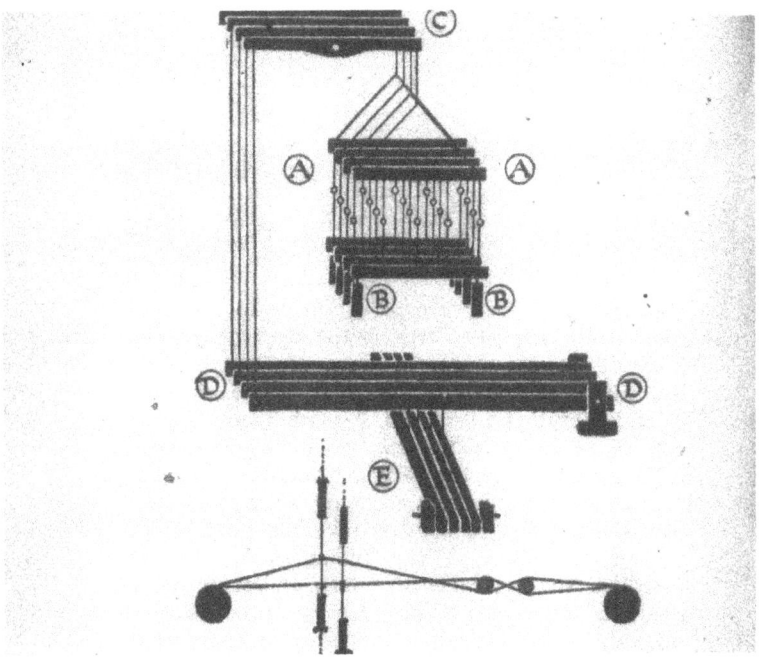

2 The term wool loft has caused some confusion by giving the impression that warping, for instance, took place up in the rafters, which cannot have been the case. When James Montagu's Charge to the Grand Jury at the Easter 1720 Quarter Sessions was printed, the word was spelled wool-lauft, perhaps indicating a dialect pronunciation.

3 Modern handloom weavers call harnesses 'shafts'. This has led to confusion.

It will be seen that from the loom in the diagram that one treadle is needed to control each harness. In the 19th century devices which made it possible for a loom with two treadles to work a number of harnesses became available. These are discussed later.

By raising and lowering the harnesses, the shed (the opening through which the shuttle is to pass) can be varied according to the weave required. An essential part of the loom is omitted from the diagram – the slay, which moving in the shed towards the weaver at the cloth beam end of the loom, pushes the weft thread hard into position after each throw of the shuttle.

The following pictures will make the arrangement of a handloom clear.

A handloom at Palmer and Mackays' Courts Mill c1900. It was probably used for pattern weaving

The weaver also had to find harnesses and slays (or reeds) for his loom.

Handloom weaving at the Esgair Moel Woollen Mill at the Welsh Folk Museum, St Fagans

A handloom at a Bradford factory c1900

[A CARD.]

"*Good Articles recommend themselves.*"

DANIEL HUNTLEY,
MORTIMER-ST., TROWBRIDGE,

REED MAKER, &c.,
BY MACHINERY,
For Weaving Woollen, Cotton, Silk,
AND ALL OTHER GOODS,
WARRANTED OF SUPERIOR QUALITY.

COTTAGE WEAVING

From the beginning of the industry until the later part of the 18th century, all weaving was done in weavers' cottages of no more than two storeys. We begin by describing the location of these in the centre of Trowbridge, and then trace the development of groups of such houses by 'settlements on the waste' of groups of houses near the town centre, then of groups in the more rural parts of the parish, and finally of such groups elsewhere in the neighbourhood. We then consider the structure of the weavers' cottages, and especially where the loom was situated. This discussion is continued into the 1860s.

IN THE TOWN

Although evidence is lacking, there can be no doubt that from the earliest days of the industry weavers carried out their work in their own homes. Thomas Long, who died in 1562, and his widow Joan, in 1583, both left money to their weavers in Trowbridge and Hilperton. At this time, of course, the built-up area of the town was very small, so that many of them even in Trowbridge parish must have lived in the rural parts. Information about housing for poor people within the town is lacking before the 18th century, when we get details both from deeds and insurance policies of sites on which some of the houses, often described as thatched, must have stood in courts behind the street. We still have Silverthorne's Court running from Roundstone Street to Duke Street, and Narrow Wine Street, formerly Cottle's Barton, off Fore Street, both of which take their names from 18th-century owners. These have survived because they are through ways.

Other courts behind houses have long since been swept away, often as a result of sanitary reforms. No. 1 Castle Street (now the Fore Street entrance to the Shires) had in 1734 several cottages behind, occupied by eight tenants. This court, later known as Cadby's Yard, was removed in the 1860s. On the site of No. 3 Castle Street stood Porter's Barton. In 1766 John Porter, cook, occupied the house on the street; behind were five houses, one thatched, occupied

The last houses in Silverthorne's Court c1950

by three shearmen, a dyer, and a labourer. By 1802 there were nine houses behind. A house on the site of 56 Fore Street had twelve tenements behind. Marshman's Yard which stood where the Market House was built can be traced from 1740. Henbest's Barton off Roundstone Street took its name from an early-18th century owner who was a carpenter. At the corner of Church Street and Silver Street three houses and five small tenements stood in 1776. In 1710 a tiler took a lease of a plot 36 feet by 30 feet in Back Street and built four tenements on it.

Although specific information is lacking, we can be sure that some

The entrance to Read's Yard, which ran through from Fore Street to what is now Church Street, sketched by Canon Jackson to show the stone with the Hungerford crest built into it. This shows that the houses were no doubt built c1731, when the materials of Farleigh Castle were put up for sale.

weaving, at least, was carried out in these courts.

The prosperity of the medley cloth industry after 1660 led to the development of two new areas, the Conigre by the Houlton family and Duke Street by the lord of the manor. Both included houses of some status, but it is clear that in both areas some of the plots granted were used to build small tenements. This is also true of The Halve; we still have a fine terrace of grand houses, but other plots were used to build yards of small cottages, now gone.

PLACES CLOSE TO THE TOWN

A COMPLETELY DIFFERENT way in which new housing became available, in this case entirely for workpeople, arose as a result of agricultural changes. When the full series of manorial records resumes in 1660, Trowbridge was still a common field manor. On either side of the town East and West Fields were divided into unfenced 'strips', farmed as they had been for centuries, by alternate cropping and fallowing. Thus we see that the fields were to be 'broken' [thrown open for pasturing animals] at certain dates and then not to be 'fed' with sheep until cattle had been fed for ten days. Breaches of these regulations were reported, and animals pounded, but such references become fewer, and we hear more and more of exchanges of lands and of new enclosures. By 1700 or before this piecemeal enclosure was complete, and farming carried on in closes or 'tinings', what we call fields today.

This left free a certain amount of land still not enclosed, typically verges of grass probably used as 'baiting places' for the plough cattle and horses to feed on. These provided tempting places for the erection of cottages. This was technically illegal – there was an Elizabethan statute against it – and encroachments by the erection of cottages diminished the area available for pasture. Manorial and parochial authorities may well have been suspicious too. So the erection of cottages on the waste was regularly presented (as an offence) at the manorial court, though apparently with little effect. In 1667, for instance, Matthew Mannings was ordered to pluck down a cottage for which he had been presented before. The next year the court was told that he and his wife were both dead, but that the cottage was still standing. Many such cottages were no doubt built by weavers.

One group of cottages that arose in this way was at the entrance into the East Field, at what was until 1977 the beginning of Hilperton Road, now only a roundabout. We know the extent of the common field at this point exactly – the strip or halve nearest to the town still remains as a street. So the gate which kept the stock in when the field was being fed stood at this point. It is called in the records variously Burds Gate or Burge [? dialect Bridge] Gate, neither name easily explained. In 1665 it was presented that Burds Gate against the corn field was 'all to pieces, down flat', and the tenant of the demesne farm was liable to repair it. In 1668 an encroachment at Burds Gate was presented. But it is not until the early 18th century that certain references to buildings appear – a house outside Burge Gate in 1710, and three cottages near Brig Gate in 1720.

In 1708 Joseph Houlton entered into a bond with Joseph Edwards, mason, guaranteeing him possession of a cottage in the East Field. When Edwards disposed of it in 1718 he simply assigned the bond to the new owner. A house, perhaps this one, outside the Burgegate was presented in 1710, and three cottages near Brig Gate in 1720.

This row consists of the successors to the cottages at Burds Gate and were demolished in 1977. A sad commentary on how much character has been lost to the needs of road traffic.

When a house which originated in this way came to be sold, the vendor could not make out a freehold title, and so conveyance was made by lease for a very long period. In the mid-18th century, a house on the site of what became No. 4 Hilperton Road was leased for 500 years. Any further sales could then be made by assigning the lease. Another way round the problem of title was not to employ a fussy lawyer at all. Two examples are illustrated. They relate to the same house. In 1754 Samuel Appleby sold a house on the waste in Hilperton Lane to Sarah Hancock for £4, a price which suggests that it was the first primitive cottage on the site. By 1770 its value had increased to £56, the sum which Benjamin Boutcher received from John Marler. Improvements included a shop window. In 1785 Enoch Beams, a weaver, bought a cottage with the broad loom in it for 40 guineas, also by a home-made deed drawn up by Job Holloway, schoolmaster. In 1805 Beams sold it to Edward Pourch pawnbroker, for £50. Marler, a bookseller, and Pourch were typical purchasers of this type of property.

The other way into the East Field was by what we now call Union Street, but no evidence of enclosure of waste there has been found.

The Seymour Estate now stands where the common field called Adcroft once lay. It was approached by a lane which had enclosed ground on both sides

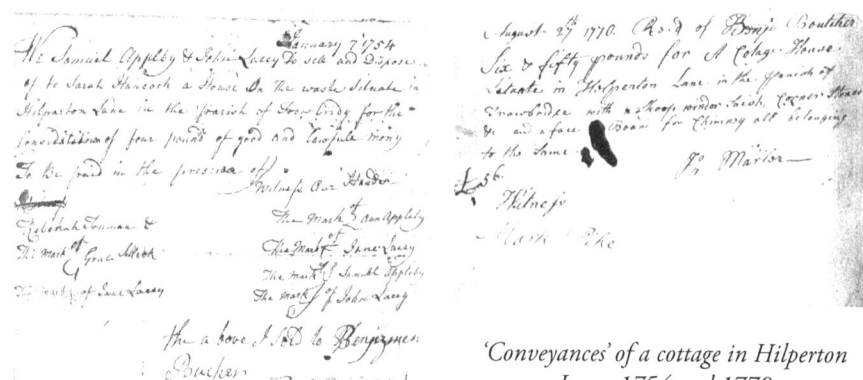

'Conveyances' of a cottage in Hilperton Lane, 1754 and 1770

until it entered the field at the top of the hill (near where the Twelve Bells pub is today), but the gate called Hill Gate stood at the bottom of the hill which today we call Shails Lane.

The earliest indication of building outside the gate comes from a copyhold admission (a document amounting to a lease by the manorial authorities) of 1585 to a new-built cottage on the waste outside Hill Gate. Another admission of 1607 was to a piece of land there which must have been near the entrance to Riverway. Successive renewals show that a group of houses developed on what was called the Plat or the Plot, later Chartist's Square. One which changed hands in 1707 stood on a piece of ground 16 ft by 14 ft, a minimal house indeed.

I imagine the lane up the hill as a wide grassy one, certainly tempting for the erection of cottages. The first presentment of one comes from Quarter Sessions in 1631, because it was straightening the highway from Trowbridge to Bradford[4] – this was actually no more than a footway, crossing the Biss by Pew Bridge, which probably stood near where Ladydown Mill was later built.

By the time we have map evidence[5] some development had begun in Shails Lane, but details of the histories of individual houses are not easy to find. A few begin with long leases, but we suspect that many changed hands without

---

4   We have throughout this book omitted our Bradford's distinguishing 'on Avon', which it only acquired in 1860. When I first began to lecture on the woollen industry more than sixty years ago, I was asked several times in Bradford if it was true that Bradford in Yorkshire was named after our Bradford. It was not, of course.

5   The map from which this and several subsequent extracts are shown was in the collection of the late Fred Pitt. It is at present in private hands but will be passed to the Wiltshire and Swindon History Centre in due course. It is only a partly-finished sketch, not dated but apparently c1775.

formal deeds. What details we have indicate poor cottages of little value. Edward Pourch, the pawnbroker, bought several here; in 1911 his Hayward descendants owned two that were in ruins and the site of one that had been demolished.

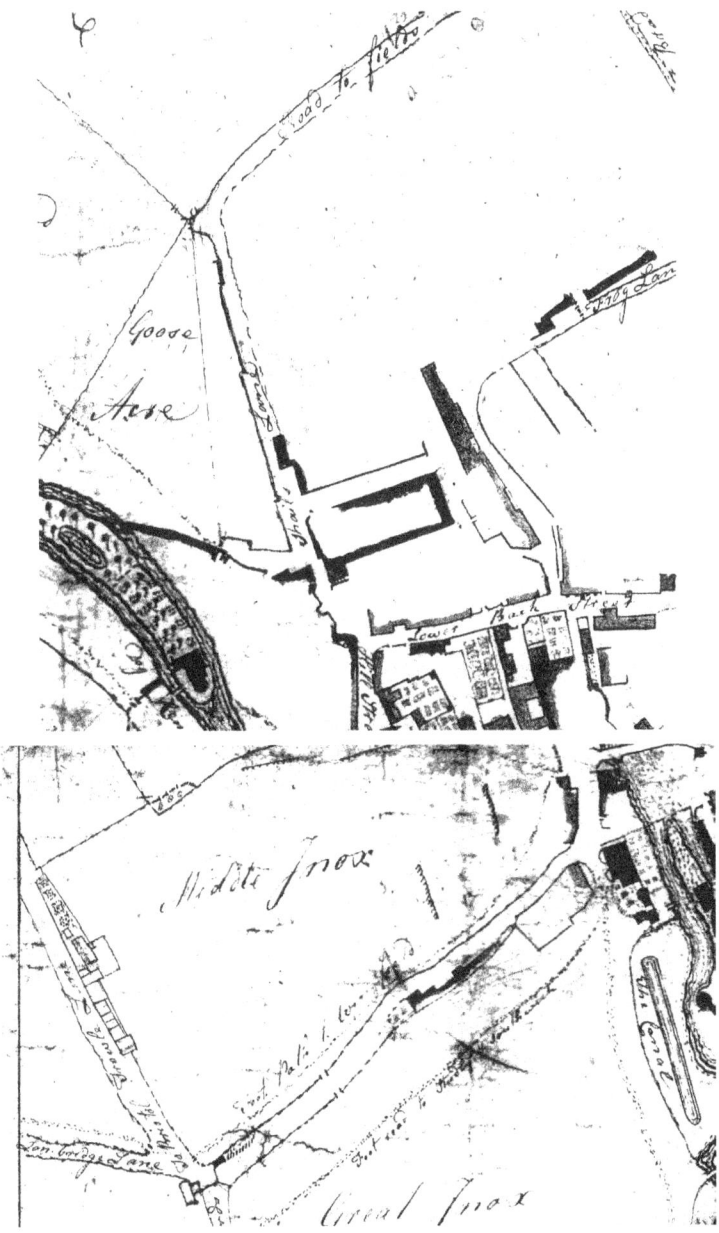

The map illustrated above shows that the 'suburb' which grew up to the west of the town, which by the end of the 18th century had filled the south side of Stallard Street with small houses as far up as the Rose and Crown, grew up in the same way. The boundary here was one of the large closes called the Innoxes. An interesting feature here was that a footpath ran inside the field behind the houses. It was entered by what is now Studley Mill yard, and ran close to the backs of the houses, so that we look down on its route from the Shires car park. The path as far as Newtown was closed by order of Quarter Sessions in 1801, but the line of the upper part of it has been preserved by a bridge over the railway and the back lane behind St. George's Terrace, coming out by the Labour Club. The path then continued to Studley on the line which later became Gloucester Road.

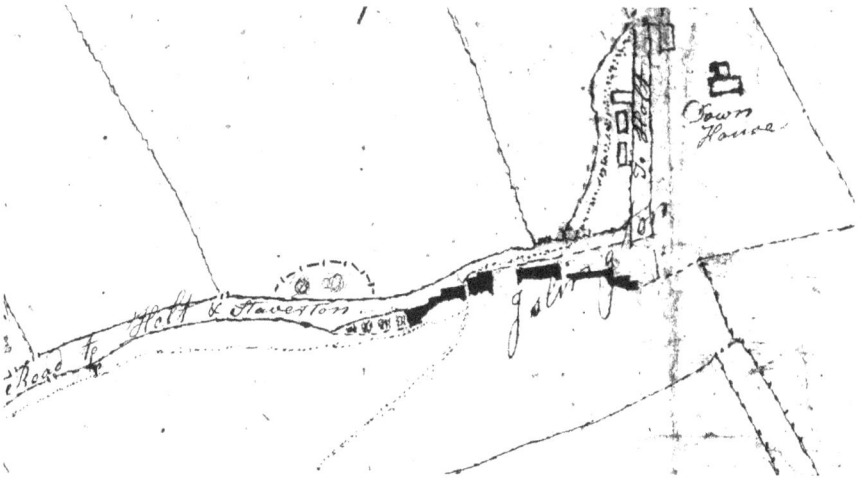

The fourth area of settlement on the waste adjoining the town was at the entrance to the common pasture called the Down. This remained open until 1809, the road to Staverton passing through it unfenced. On the final sale of the manorial property in that year it was divided up and sold in lots, the common rights having been extinguished in some way. No building took place within the gate, which must have stood near, and been replaced by, the turnpike gate after 1769. The cottages were built on waste opposite what is now Palmer Gardens and adjoining houses, and round the corner on the west side of the road up to the gate.

The first indication comes from 1704, when two men were presented for cottages near Down gate; the same two were presented again in 1711. As we saw in Hilperton Road, the best evidence comes from later in the century, when original builders or their successors were selling their houses. A good example comes from 1773, when Edward Cox, mason, paid £10 3s. 6d. for a three-thousand year lease of a ruinous and decayed house which stood near the entrance to a close called Downhayes. Other houses changed hands for £10 and £20, and thousand-year leases have been noted from 1782, 1785, and 1793.

Looking at the map above, there is a gap just above the I of Islington; Timbrell Street was later built through this gap. The cottages to the left of the gap were later demolished and Prospect Place built. However, the cottages had been built on the waste outside the field boundary, but Prospect Place was built a little further south and inside the field boundary on land owned by the Timbrell family.

The name Islington was evidently current by this time. We can only suppose that someone familiar with London nicknamed the settlement north of Trowbridge, and the name stuck.

Andrews and Dury's map of Wiltshire 1773. This shows Islington and the Down well, but note how they failed with the centre of the town.

This house with weaver's windows still stands on the west side of Islington. Its exact history is not known.

THE OUTER PARTS OF THE PARISH

THE STUDLEYS

THE PART OF Trowbridge parish west of the Biss was the tithing of Studley. Although it included the West common field, much of it had been cleared and enclosed into closes in the Middle Ages. Some of these were farmed from copyhold or freehold houses at scattered places throughout the tithing – Galley Farm, Holbrook Farm, and Drynham Farm, to name but three, were all active in my own lifetime. Access to the farms and their lands was by grassy lanes, which formed part of the 'waste' of the manor, and so were controlled by the manorial court. In 1660, for instance, it was ordered 'that none was to put any sheep into Studley's lanes except it be between washing and shearing, which is but three suns'. But, as we have seen, farming was changing, and the lanes provided tempting verges for the erection of cottages, groups of which grew up at several places.

The nearest to the town was at the junction where the roads to Bradford, Wingfield and North Bradley ran off in different directions near the present

Trinity Church, not so easy to visualize now owing to the modern road system there. John Stallard was among 18 men presented at the manorial court in 1660 for having built cottages on the waste. Five years later it was reported that he had sold part of a little piece of waste ground by his house to John Bull, who was about to build a cottage on it. For some reason it was Stallard's name that stuck; there can be few such obscure people commemorated by a street name today. By the time we get map evidence in 1803 there were houses near

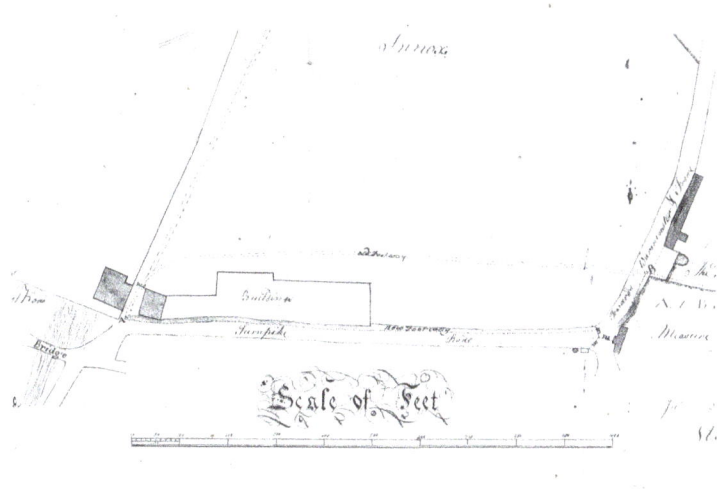

These little buildings stand as yet near the end of Gloucester Road. Each has a single room with a fireplace. Are they cottages on the waste? Or weaving shops? We understand that a new use has been found for them so that an unusual piece of Trowbridge's history will be preserved.

this point both on the way to Bradford (Trowle Lane), and at the beginning of what we now call Newtown. In 1804 two cottages near the Turnpike Gate were sold for £45.

Three hamlets took the name of Studley – Lower, Middle, and Upper. The name Lower Studley, my native place, still had some currency to its inhabitants before the war. It was in contrast to Upper Studley, only in the thirties ceasing to be a separate village by the advance of housing up the Frome Road. But Middle Studley would have meant nothing to us.

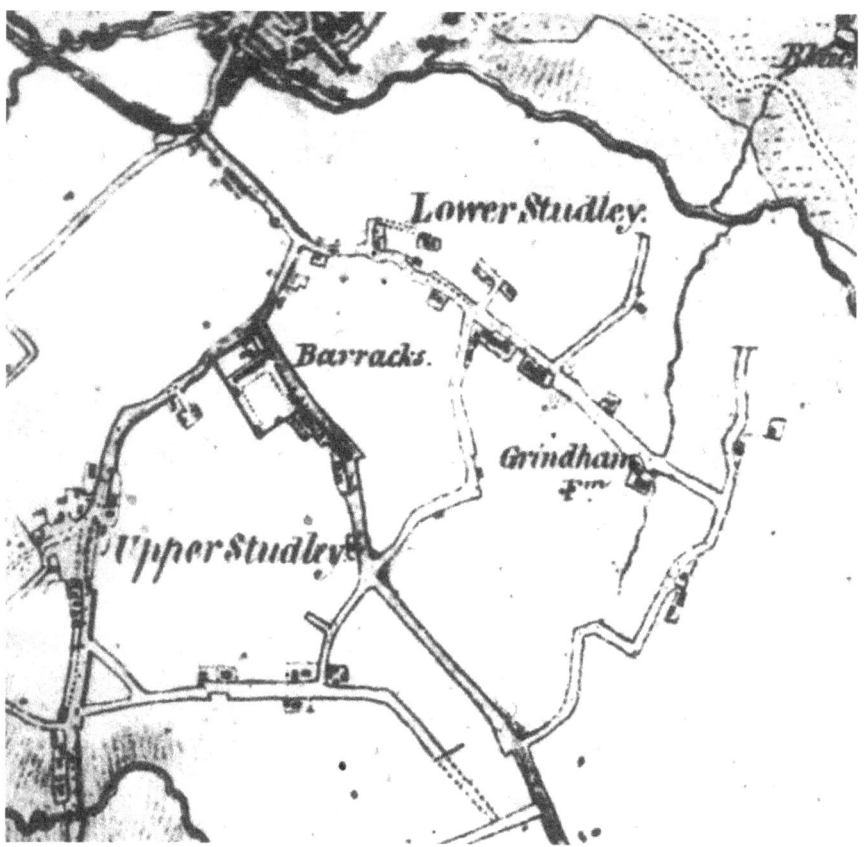

Lower Studley comprised what is now Dursley Road, Drynham Road, and the adjoining part of Holbrook Lane. A cottage built on the waste in Holbrook Lane was granted by copy of court roll in 1606. The 1803 map shows cottages on the east side of Dursley Road, the west side of Drynham Road, and the south side of Holbrook Lane. What title deeds are available show a familiar pattern of disposal to tradesmen in the town of houses of minimal value.

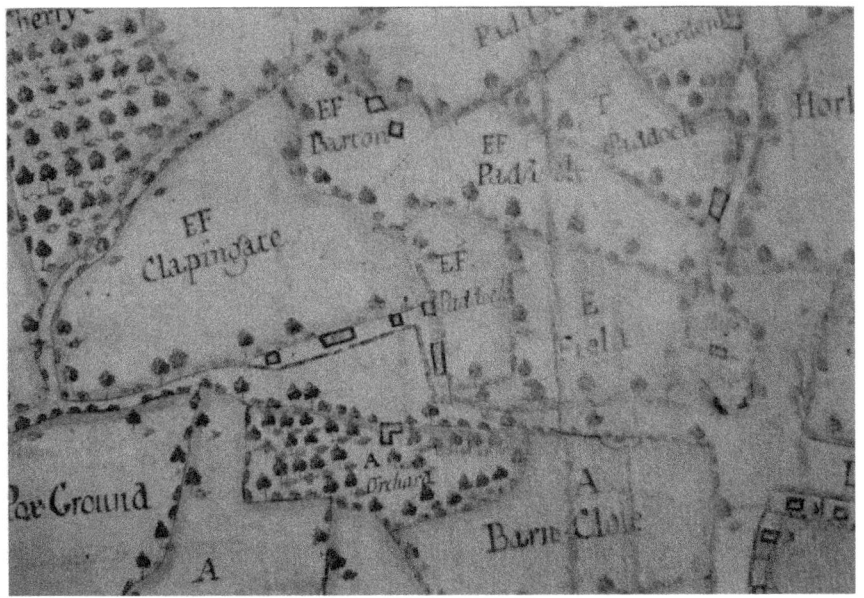

Dursley Lane, c 1775, showing cottages built round a small triangular green. This would be more or less opposite where Rutland Crescent is today.

Cottages on the verge in Drynham and Holbrook Lane (on the left hand side of the map), 1775

The original width of the lane can still be seen in Drynham Road. The garden walls of the terrace on the east mark the boundary on that side. Outside it was a verge, of which grassy patches remained, the rest being 'hard standing' (very useful to park cars) until 1971, when it was tidied up. On the west side the boundary was close behind the houses which replaced older cottages in late Victorian times.

In Holbrook Lane one cottage remained long enough for me to photograph it. There are several references to weavers called Harford living in Studley in the 17th and 18th centuries. William Harford took a North Bradley apprentice as early as 1635, and there are records of nine apprenticeships to a man (or men) between 1713 and 1758. James Bodman, in his *History of Trowbridge* of 1814, tells us 'But the most noted family, or case of antiquity of a family, is the Harford's. This family lived in Studley about the year 1650, and it is very remarkable that the house have not changed the name of its occupier and proprietor ... from that time to the present'. It may have been the one illustrated above. The first that we know is that in 1777 Richard Harford, broadweaver, succeeded his father William, and mortgaged the house; the deed spells his name in the dialect form Harvett, but Richard signed Harford. Weavers of the same name lived in the house between 1821 and 1861.

Although there is no photograph apart from one showing Ken and his twin brother prepared for an Arctic expedition on a summer afternoon, he had a clear memory of the cottage further up the lane in which his maternal grandparents lived until it was demolished in 1937. It had only one room below and one bedroom reached by a stair which went straight into it, protected only by a rail. Water and lavatory were only reached by going outside to the back. If it had had even a narrow loom in it, living space would have been very limited. In fact, between 1821 and 1851 it was occupied by a man 'of independent means'.

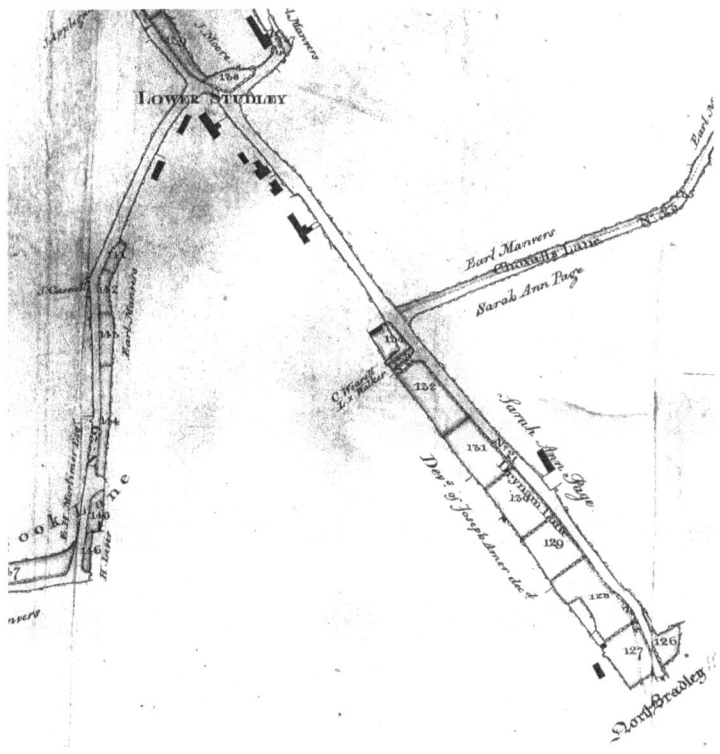

Shortly after Thomas Timbrell became lord of the manor in 1809 an Enclosure Act was obtained; the award, made in 1818, enclosed such of the remaining verges in the Studley area as were worth bothering with. In

Drynham the verge beyond the cottages was made into small pieces of garden size which would have made good building plots, but in fact no more houses were built.

In Dursley Road an allotment under the award adjoined the path through the fields (now taken over the railway by a footbridge), and these houses were built on it. They were occupied by weaving families called Dunford.

The other parts of Studley comprised, like Lower Studley, a mixture of old farm sites, cottages on the waste, and cottages built either to live in or to let. They can be dealt with more briefly, mostly by illustrations.

Middle Studley comprised groups of houses on the lower part of Frome Road and at places on Bradley Road, where some cottages stand near the entrance to College Road.

Whether they originated as cottages on the waste is not clear. The cottages illustrated stood on the south side of Frome Road not far from the Ship pub and opposite Park Street School. They are being demolished as part of a Civil Defence exercise in 1936.

By the 1818 award long thin strips on either side of the road to North Bradley were allotted to Thomas Timbrell, and later maps show that they were planted with trees. Just before the road left the parish, the award map shows a building on the west side. At this point now stand Timbrell Cottages. They bear Timbrell's coat of arms, and look as though they were intended for almshouses. In 1841, however, all three were occupied by weavers, and why they were built like this remains a mystery.

Cottages at Cuckoo's Corner, Bradley Road, opposite the entrance to the Croft

There were several old manorial farms in Upper Studley, which we now call Studley Green. Cottages were built on verges, and round a small green. A mortgage of a cottage made by a thousand-year lease in 1828 said that it stood on ground enclosed many years ago out of the waste.

This picture was taken about 1900 in Upper Studley. The exact location is not known.

Several cottages still stand facing Frome Road. These are almost opposite the Black Horse pub.

Others have gone

Whiterow. Some of what is shown is modern infilling, joining up old cottages and very nicely done

Beyond Studley Green was a separate group called Whiterow. This is named in a Turnpike Act as White Trough. This error can be explained by a misunderstanding of local dialect. When Ken was a boy he, and most people he knew, being dialect speakers, never pronounced trough as 'troff', but always as always 'trow'. Therefore Whiterow was interpreted as White Trough by the drafters of the Act.

Several cottages, built on the verge in Silver Street Lane, have gone without trace and no pictures are known to survive. They are shown on the 1774 map above.

HILPERTON MARSH

WE HAVE SEEN above that no cottages were built actually within the common called the Down. But the farmers of Staverton, part of Trowbridge manor, had rights in a common called Weeke or Wyke Marsh. A copyhold grant of a cottage built on it was made in 1633, and it is likely that cottages at Staverton presented from time to time were on plots enclosed out of it. This common adjoined one belonging to Hilperton, and the considerable settlement which grew up here became known as Hilperton Marsh. Squatters on such commons had, of course, no common rights, but they were probably able to pasture a donkey or a few geese without interference – that is, until the common was enclosed by the award of 1818.

First edition Ordnance Survey one inch map, 1817. The map shows a series of cottages along the southern edge of the common. On enclosure in 1818, the new road we now call Horse Road was made some distance in front of this group so that on its southern side the older cottages have newer houses between them and the road. Another group south of the King's Arms are also shown but had been demolished by 1887.

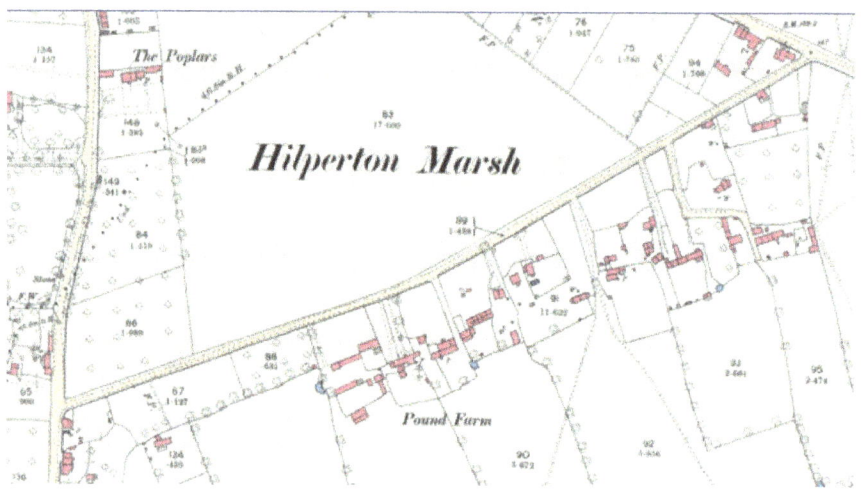

In 1818, Horse Road was laid out across the common, leaving the cottages well away from the new road. This map, surveyed in 1884, shows that they were reached through a series of lanes.

Old cottages on the south side of Horse Road

NEARBY VILLAGES

STEEPLE ASHTON PARISH

EQUALLY TEMPTING WERE the extensive commons belonging to the manor of Steeple Ashton. This then included Semington, West Ashton, North Bradley, and Southwick. The extent of the common land before enclosure in the early 19th century is best shown on a map (overleaf).

A survey of 1604 lists 55 cottages on the waste naming locations, some still appearing on modern maps, such as Yarnbrook, Brokerswood, Lambert's Marsh, and Kettle Lane. A more elaborate enquiry made in 1637 gives the names of 138 'coottedgerrs'. It is less specific about location except they stretched from Brokerswood to Semington, but tells us how much ground they had – hardly ever more than a few lugs [perches] – and how long they had been erected. A frequent age, and the longest given, is sixty years, which presumably meant 'time out of mind'. Many were more recent. Some had been built with the consent of the parish or the lord. Many were held 'upon good behaviour'.

Two now-disappeared groups of cottages lay in the common between West Ashton and Trowbridge. The 1604 survey of Steeple Ashton mentions John Silverthorne being at Dodsmead Corner, which stood near Biss Wood and was generally known as Blackball. After this there are references to Silverthornes of Black Ball in the parish registers and wills.

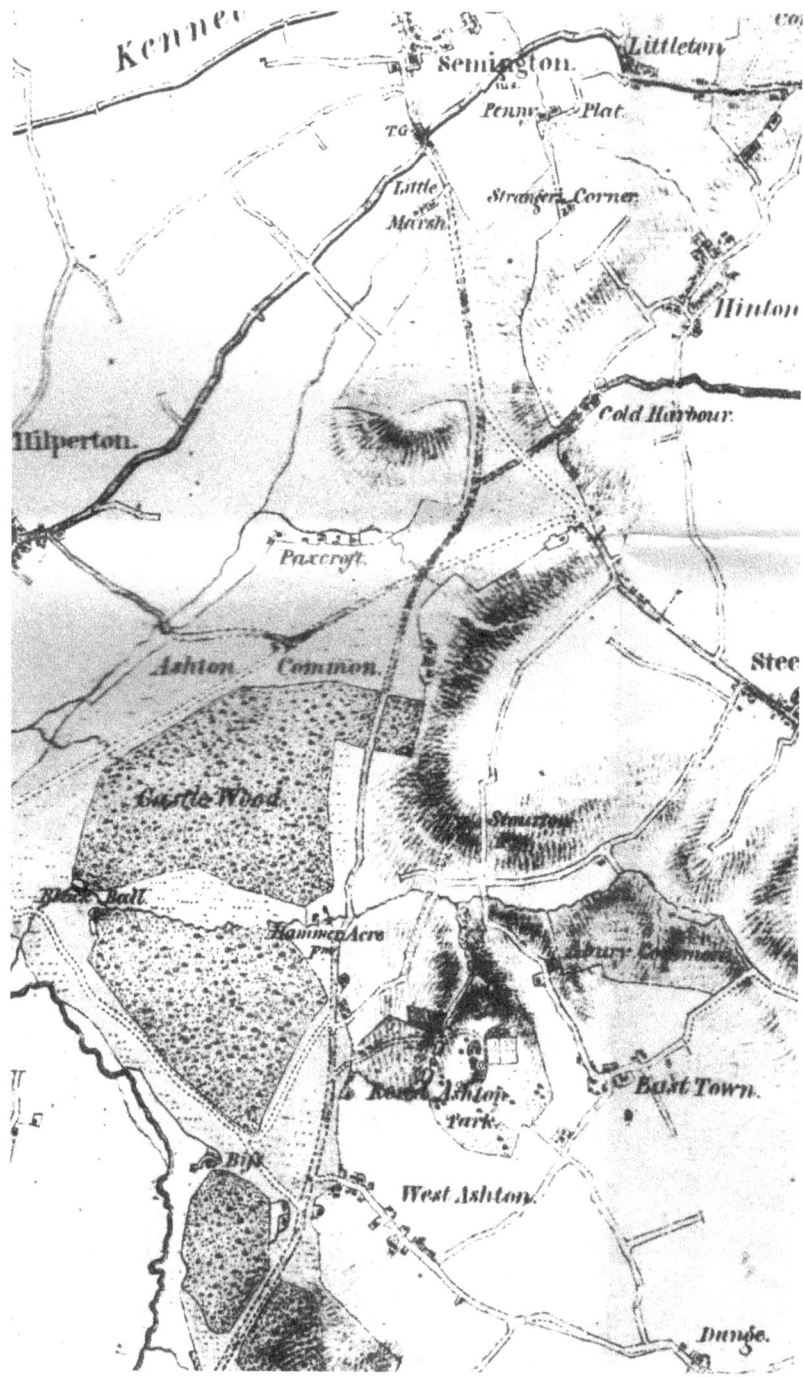

OS 1st edition 1" 1817. Several settlements on the waste are shown – Black Ball, Biss, Paxcroft and Coldharbour.

Wiltshire Hearth Tax returns are notoriously incomplete but we are lucky that the 1673 certificate of exemptions survives in the Martyn family papers. It includes the names of those whose houses have 'not above two chymneyes, fire hearths or stoves'. Most of these were in groups, separated by lines, in a list headed 'Cottages upon the common waste or highways'. Of these we can be fairly sure that a group of seven houses, of which four were occupied by Silverthornes, was at Black Ball. The other five groups cannot be firmly placed though one must have been at Biss, another at Yarnbrook and one near the present crossroads at the top of the hill at West Ashton. We should note here that Andrews and Dury's 1773 map, in a rare mistake, mixes up Black Ball and Biss.

As they came up for sale cottages at Black Ball and Biss were bought by the Longs of Rood Ashton and pulled down. Some of the inhabitants were re-housed in the estate cottages in the village. Black Ball had completely gone by 1887 and only one building remained at Biss.

NORTH BRADLEY AND SOUTHWICK

NORTH BRADLEY AND Southwick were classic weaving villages. As A. Farquharson wrote in his history of North Bradley in 1881, the weaving trade was carried on in nearly every cottage.

Beside the villages, there was ample common land, Steeple Ashton continuing near both villages to Rode itself (until 1936 the part of that village called Rode Hill was in Wiltshire). A number of groups of cottages on the waste can be seen – Yarnbrook, Scotland, Ireland and Brokerswood.

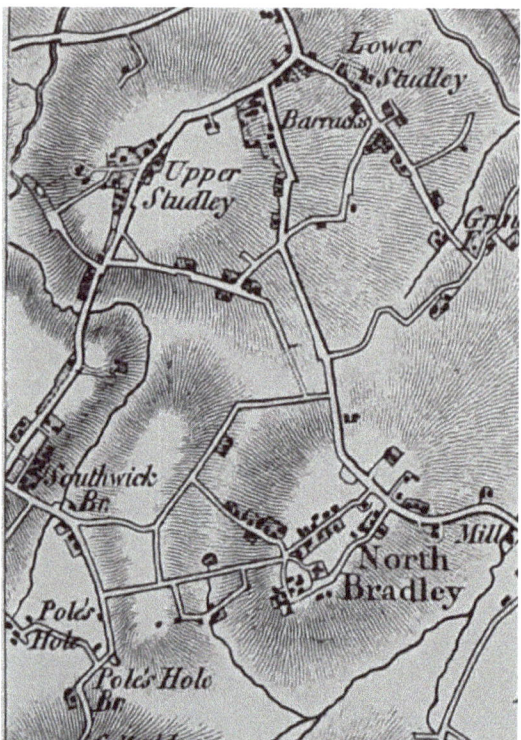

Ordnance Survey 1" map, first edition 1817. The scattered nature of the settlements is evident

A house on the Yarnbrook Road in North Bradley. The long weaver's window has been partly blocked.

This cottage still stands on the main road through Southwick but is no longer thatched

Advertisement for cottages at Warp Lane, Southwick, held for a term of 1,000 years beginning in 1795.

DILTON MARSH

Like Hilperton Marsh, the name of another classic weaving village, Dilton Marsh, betrays its origin.

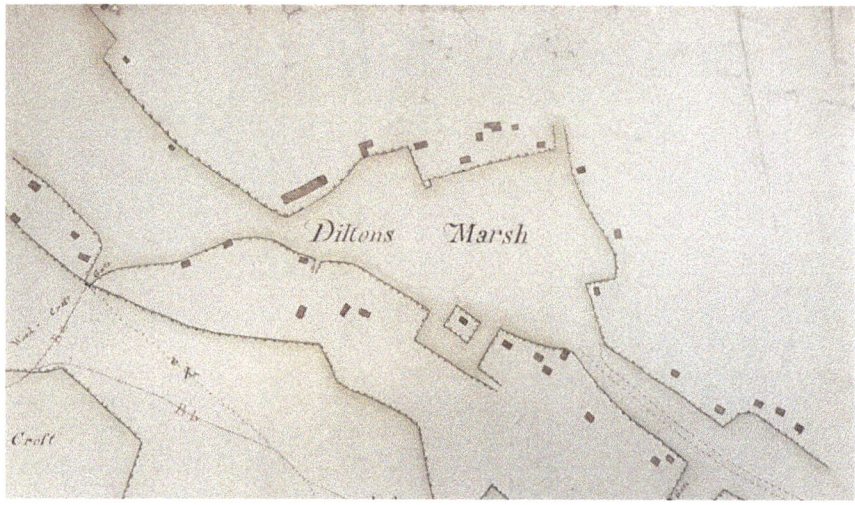

This is a map of 1778. The Marsh is at a considerable distance from the church and original settlement, and by the eighteenth century was much larger. As we have seen elsewhere, waste land around the edge of the common was gradually settled. The common land was enclosed in 1802.

Andrews and Dury map 1773

As we shall see below, many weavers in Dilton Marsh worked for Trowbridge clothiers. In 1861 the census enumerator in Dilton Marsh was careful to note that people were handloom weavers (there was only one power loom weaver in the village). In all there were 57 householders who were weavers, of whom 29 had other family members working with them, 107 handloom weavers in the village in all. This was a much higher proportion of handloom weavers than would have been seen in the towns at the time.

This old postcard shows the scattered nature of the settlement in Dilton Marsh. All the buildings shown must have originated as cottages on the waste.

WHAT WERE THE WEAVERS' HOUSES LIKE?

THE WEAVER'S COTTAGE had to accommodate not only a loom but also nearby a 'quilling turn' on which were wound the bobbins called quills for the shuttle. This was carried out by an assistant, almost always a child. The picture on p. 99 shows a tableau in the Frome Jubilee celebrations of 1897 depicting the methods of weaving at the start of Victoria's reign.

The cottages built by the original settlers on the waste must have been of simple construction, which would have been necessary owing to the haste with which they were put up. This arose from a widespread belief that if a cottage could be erected over one day it would give the freehold title. Joe Bettey, in his *Rural Life in Wessex,* gives a vivid picture of the erection of such a one-day cottage in Dorset. It was reported to the Lord of the Manor that the man had already made-up frames for the house and had straw on the site. He would also no doubt have arranged for his friends and neighbours to provide the necessary help to get the job done in time. It was felt necessary for the successful completion of such a cottage that smoke should be rising from the chimney by evening, so a chimney assured the significance in the operation, and was if possible built first by a professional bricklayer or mason. Once the smoke was rising it was felt that the title was complete. The late Avril Tadd told me that relatives in Nomansland near Salisbury had, still standing in the garden of their house, the chimney of an older house which they said gave them title to the house.

This cottage at Radstock, though it only stood four feet high to the eaves, had a large chimney. One-night cottages were actually illegal by law. A statute of 1589 forbade the erection of cottages unless they had four acres of land to go with them. Any encroachment on a common could be held to diminish the common rights of the farmers entitled to use them. We have seen above the manorial authorities of Trowbridge and Steeple Ashton being concerned about such cottages, and we can imagine the overseers of the poor might be worried that new settlers might in due course be a burden on the poor rates to which they did not contribute. In our area, however, there can have been no serious effort to deter the erection of cottages or to remove them when built. It was probably felt that a cottager ejected could become an immediate burden to the parish, and that weavers were needed to meet the needs of the industry.

This print is of a weaver's cottage on the Scottish island of Islay in 1772 but gives us a plausible picture of what a first-generation cottage in our area may have been like before improvement.

WEAVING SHOPS WITHIN COTTAGES

ALTHOUGH WEAVING SHOPS are regularly mentioned in wills and deeds, it is not easy to determine their relationship to the structure of the weaver's house – whether they were part of the main house, an extension or lean-to, or even a separate building.

An extension or separate building is suggested, for instance, when in 1611 Henry Ladd of Chippenham left money to a son 'when he shall build a shop for a loom and not before.' In 1687 John Burges, a Studley weaver, left £5 'to build my son Henry Burges a shop for his loom'. In 1709 Anne Willis of North Bradley left the part of her house called the weaving shop separately from the rest. In 1719 Roger Callaway of Bratton, broadweaver, left 'my shoop that is joyned unto my house that I now lives in'. In 1736 a Seend weaver went out of his loom into his dwellinghouse.

This cottage which once stood in the High Street in Chapmanslade appears to show how a room was extended forward to provide a weaver's window.

The phrasing of deeds and advertisements often suggests that the weaving shop was an appendage to the house rather than an integral part of it. In 1781, for instance, two freehold tenements adjoining each other near Rode Common with two weaving shops belonging to them were for sale. A lease of a house in Studley in 1781 includes a provision that the owner shall 'ceile' the chamber over the weaving shop. A 1787 advertisement is for four cottages at Turleigh with weaver's shops for two broadlooms each. In 1793 several houses at Studley were described as having weaving shops 'adjoining' or 'belonging'. Another sale at Studley in 1809 was of a cottage and two-loom weaving shop and a cottage and one-loom weaving shop.

Probate inventories can also be an important source. Of fifteen inventories of weavers abstracted in Ivor Slocombe's recent edition of pre-1700 Bradford inventories, two indicate that the weaving was done in the main part of the house – one in a shop with a chamber [bedroom] over it, and one in an inner chamber. Three mention shops containing looms, and one a shop without mention of a loom. Three mention looms but with no indication where they were. The rest mention neither shop nor loom. Two early examples come from Trowbridge; John Marshman, 1608, with a loft over the shop, and William Bull, 1616, with a chamber over it. The 1698 inventory of Nathaniel Long of Hilperton refers to the house; it consisted of a kitchen and a shop containing two broad looms on the ground floor, and a kitchen chamber and a shop chamber above.

From 1856 we get good details from newspaper advertisements about the arrangement of the cottages. The best information of all comes from the sale books of the Trowbridge auctioneer George Snailum (WSHC 738) from 1865 onwards, which contain the detailed notes on the properties he was selling. Details are worth quoting in full (dimensions to the nearest foot):

1856	Hilperton Marsh	Parlour, kitchen, large shop for four narrow looms, three bedrooms over
1856	Hoopers Pool, Southwick	House formerly let as one cottage, now as two; large shop for six looms, two kitchens, two sculleries, four bedrooms over
1856	Southwick	Two weaving shops, two bedrooms over
1857	Whiterow, Trowbridge	Sitting room, parlour, large weaving shop for four broad looms, brewhouse, five bedrooms
1857	Whiterow, Trowbridge adjoining	Kitchen, weaving shop, two bedrooms
1857	Silver Street Lane, Trowbridge	Sitting room, weaving shop, two bedrooms
1865	Ireland, North Bradley	Kitchen 16x10, weaving shop 17x17 for two broad looms, three bedrooms over
1865	Green Lane, Southwick	Living room 16x16 for two narrow looms, two bedrooms over
1867	Silver Street Lane, Trowbridge	Lane Sitting room 15x11, weaving shop 16x10 for two narrow looms, two bedrooms same size over
1867	Woodmarsh, North Bradley	Sitting room 11x9, weaving shop 14x9, two bedrooms same size over
1867	Church Lane, North Bradley	Weaving shop 16x9 for one narrow loom, large pantry, one bedroom over
1867	Church Lane, North Bradley	Sitting room 16x12, weaving shop 15x17, wash house, bedrooms over
1867	Church Lane, North Bradley	Sitting room and weaving shop

1867	The Rank, North Bradley	Sitting room 13x11, weaving shop 17x16 for four looms, one bedroom over sitting room, two over shop
1867	Axe and Cleaver, North Bradley	Sitting room 10x9, workshop for a broad loom 13x12, two bedrooms over, one used as a workshop for a broad loom
1867	Axe and Cleaver, North Bradley	Sitting room 17x10, workshop 16x16 for two broad looms, two bedrooms over the weaving shop both equal to it in size
1869	Southwick	Living room, weaving shop for four narrow looms, two bedrooms over
1869	Southwick	Living room, weaving shop for six narrow looms, two bedrooms over
1870	Southwick	Front parlour, large weaving shop, and two good bedrooms with landing
1870	Southwick	Front room 10x9, weaving shop 13x13 fitted with oven and grate, bedrooms over each, coal hole, pantry
1870	Southwick	Parlour 11x12, passage, weaving shop 12x12, landing and bedroom over parlour, bedroom over shop
1870	Southwick	Living room 12x14, weaving shop 17x16 for three narrow looms with stone floor and four windows, three bedrooms over
1871	Dymott Square, Hilperton	Parlour, workshop for three narrow looms, three bedrooms over
1872	Warp Lane, Southwick	Parlour 12x9, weaving shop 19x13, three bedrooms over

Apart from three minimal houses at Green Lane, Southwick, Church Lane, North Bradley, and Southwick (1856), all these examples suggest that the village weaver had a living room separate from his shop and two or three bedrooms upstairs.

THE THREE-STOREYED WEAVERS' HOUSES

I NOW GO on to consider a particular problem, that of the three-storeyed house, the top storey often (though by no means always) with what appears to be a wide workshop-type window. During the period 1790 – 1830 the population of Trowbridge doubled in size, from about 5,000 to almost 11,000, and several hundred new houses were built. These included terraces of such houses in several places. In the frenzy to replace 'substandard' housing in the 1950s and 1960s, some good groups were swept away, but we still have terraces in Yerbury Street, Castle Street and Newtown. These have attracted the attention of industrial archaeologists as being weaver's houses, a description which we question in this section. We should point out here that we have excluded The Halve, where building plots became available from *c.* 1780. The remaining houses of three storeys with attics where of middle class rather than artisan status.

We start by drawing a contrast between Trowbridge and Bradford.

In Bradford's Newtown area, developed in the late 17th century and

early 18th century we see a new type of house, essentially of three storeys, the top one being formed by making a dormer almost as wide as two lower floors, and bringing it forward to the line of the frontage. It is hard not to believe that this was adopted unless it was to provide space for some domestic industrial activity such as weaving.

This type was never adopted in Trowbridge, and indeed at this period there were no three-storeyed houses in the town except for the largest of the clothiers' houses. The following examples will show that the houses were of two main storeys, and if the roof space was utilised at all, it was only lighted by small dormers set well back. The most that was done was to bring the small dormers forward to the eaves.

The Conigre, Trowbridge, c1890 showing a house of the type described above

Church Street, Trowbridge

Duke Street, Trowbridge. The dormers in the large house have been brought forward, which is only seen in a few examples. The Trowbridge examples are exactly contemporary with the Newtown area of Bradford.

I can think of no particular reason why this difference should occur. The two towns were making the same product at the time (medley broadcloth).

It has always been usual to consider the three-storeyed type as weaver's houses, the top floor being the workshop. However, as we will attempt to demonstrate below, the majority of weavers lived and worked in two-storey buildings. We should also note at this point that the spinning jenny was also introduced at just this time and that it is known that the small jennies of this period could be used in domestic circumstances.

Efforts to determine whether the top-floor workshops were actually used for weaving are fraught with difficulties. The building of both the Timbrell Street and Mortimer Street areas was generally achieved by the two landowning families selling off plots sufficient for one or more, but usually not more than four, houses to men in the building trade; they would build the houses, and usually quite quickly sell them on. But the purchasers were not by any means always the persons who were living, or were going to live, in the houses. They were rather more likely to be 'investors' – tradesmen in the town who intended to rent out their houses for income. Deeds of houses in both areas survive in some profusion, because the sites were purchased in the 1950s and 1960s for clearance, but even when the run goes back to the building period, they are only occasionally specific about tenants, and even if they do name them do not state their occupations, rather than the owners. Therefore, title deeds are of limited use in determining what a house was used for.

The first complete picture of where weavers lived and worked in Trowbridge comes from the 1841 census, which predates the introduction of the power loom in the area. We can therefore be sure that every weaver mentioned was a handloom weaver. Even in 1851, only five power loom weavers are recorded in the town.

Even census data of the period is not always straightforward as some streets had not yet been allocated with door numbers. It might at first sight seem easy to work back from the numbered streets of 1881 through 1871, 1861, and 1851 to 1841, but in fact it is full of pitfalls. Divided houses counted as two or three, failure to note that houses were in courts, and the kaleidoscopic changes between censuses, so that in a whole street the great majority of surnames are different every ten years, have made it very difficult to identify most weaver's-type houses with complete certainty. All we have been able to do is present a few indications, some of them negative. We have used the term weaving family to denote households in which the householder and one or more members of his or her family were weavers, because it seems most likely that in such families the weaving was done at home. Many householder weavers without other family weavers also must have worked at home, but this category may have included some journeymen who went elsewhere to a master, and also weavers who worked in shops in the factories. The same is true of households where only the wife was a weaver, and even more of weavers not family members, and put down as lodgers – but some of these could have rented a room with a loom! The lodger category we have had to treat as if they were family members.

I begin with the Timbrell Street area. Timbrell Street was begun in 1814 and had uniform rows of three-storeyed houses for its whole length but the adjoining streets such as Thomas Street, Charlotte Street and Prospect Place, had similar houses mixed with others of only two storeys.

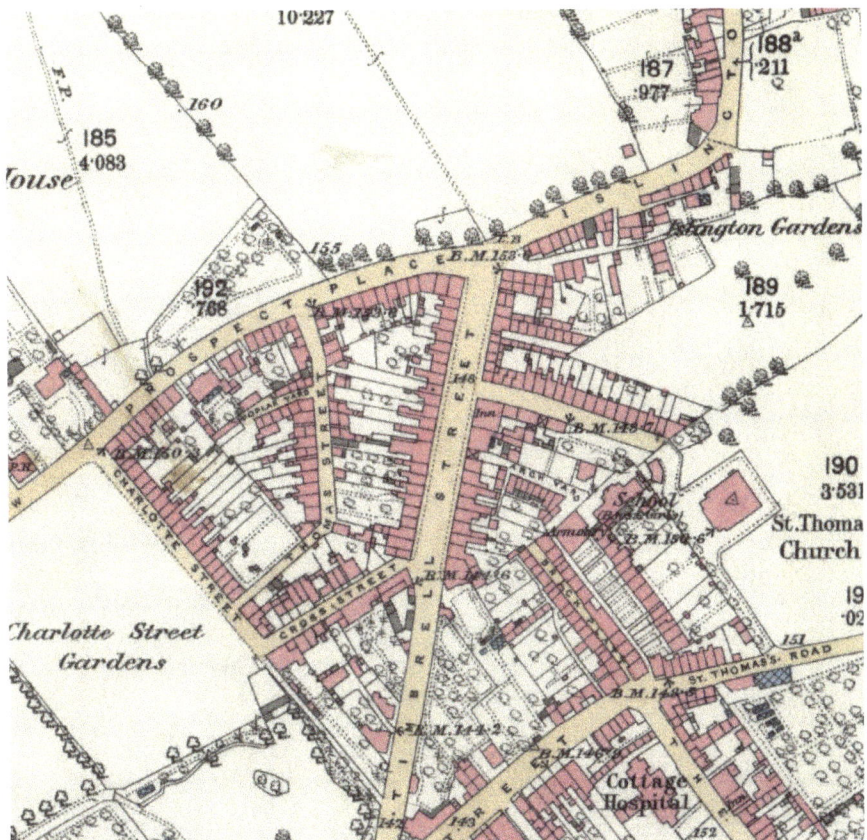

TIMBRELL STREET, west side:
    Five 1821 tenants can be identified as weavers:
    James Pitman owned two adjoining houses, occupied by six families.
    William Trapnell owned a house only occupied by his own family.

Timbrell Street complete in 1905. Note the trees.

The west side from the Prospect Place end. In the 1950s several houses at this end still had stone tiles.

The rear of the west side of Timbrell Street during demolition in the 1960s

Another view of the rear of the west side of Timbrell Street.

William Holwell owned a house occupied by two families.
Samuel Pitman occupied two adjoining house occupied by two families.
John Batchelor owned a house occupied by two families.
By 1841 still there were these weavers:
James Pitman with two lodger weavers.
Ann widow of William Trapnell.
William Holwell with a daughter.
Edward Pitman.
Also on this side were:
James Allen with a son.
Benjamin Angle.
Robert Deverall.
So in 1841 seven out of the 26 houses in this uniform row were occupied by weavers.

TIMBRELL STREET, east side

Timbrell Street east side. This group of four pairs of back to back houses stood above the entrance to York Place. They were demolished around 1960.

On this side were several courts which cannot be separated in the census from the nineteen houses fronting the street. The houses in the courts are unlikely to have been of more than two storeys. The most we can say is that in 1841 eight out of 50 houses were occupied by weavers, only one of the eight a weaving family.

PROSPECT PLACE

Prospect Place – a walk down the street from the Timbrell Street end c1960. The third and fourth pictures show the entrance to Thomas Street.

Prospect Place only had houses on its south-west side. Leaving aside three 'better' houses, it consisted of twenty-four houses of which eleven were of the three-storeyed type. In 1841 there was only one householder weaver (in one of the three-storeyed type), one wife, and one lodger, so three houses occupied by weavers in the whole twenty-four houses.

THOMAS STREET

Four pictures of Thomas Street proceeding from Prospect Place taken about 1960. In the third picture, the house numbered 4 in 1863 was put up for sale; it was the one nearest the camera on this picture. It had a parlour, entrance passage, kitchen, and scullery on the ground floor, two bedrooms on the first floor, and a weaving shop for two looms and another bedroom on the second floor. The occupier, Samuel Adlam, was a weaver in the 1861 census.

The west side had an interesting alternation of seven two- and six three-storeyed houses, almost as if they had been built to order. On the east side were six two-storeyed houses and a group of four three-storeyed houses built back to back, two facing the street and two facing backwards. In 1841 in the whole street there was a total of nine weaver householders, three of them weaving families. In two more households the wife was a weaver. They cannot be allotted to individual houses. There was a higher proportion of weavers in Prospect Place than in the adjoining streets.

CHARLOTTE STREET

This only had houses on the west side, twenty-three in all, mainly of two storeys, but with six of three storeys at three different points. There was only one weaver, a wife, in the whole street in 1841.

COBOURG PLACE AND ISLINGTON GARDENS

These were the names of groups of houses built on land behind the upper end of the east side of Timbrell Street and the lower part of Islington. Nothing is recorded of their construction. The 1886 map suggests that they were mainly small and some built back-to-back. Of the forty householders recorded in 1841, only three were weavers, one of whom, an eighty-year-old man, wove with his fifty-year-old son. They were demolished shortly before the second world war and there are no known surviving photographs.

CROSS STREET

Only nine householders were recorded in 1841, at least two of them in the large, prosperous houses on the south side also known as Timbrell Place. There was one weaver householder.

YORK BUILDINGS

No weaver lived in these 18 two-storeyed houses in 1841. They survived until at least the 1970s.

ISLINGTON

As we have seen, this street originated as groups of houses built on the waste verges at the entrance to the common called Trowbridge Down. Late 18th century maps show them facing north (now opposite Palmer Gardens) and

The row facing Palmer Gardens has been much altered, especially by the erection of a gothic Sunday school. It still includes a block of three storey buildings, now much altered and groups of two storey buildings at either end.

Above and overleaf: These terraces stood between what is now the entrance to Delamere Road and the thatched turnpike house in Islington. They survived until the 1960s.

on the west side as the road curves round. These would have been typically occupied by weavers, and indeed we know that the family of Edward Coombs, a prosperous weaver, owned several houses in the north-facing group.

Shortly after Timbrell Street was built, two terraces of houses were built on the east side, all of two storeys, and known from later advertisements to have had a living room and kitchen below and two bedrooms above. In 1841 nine of these 15 houses were occupied by weavers, seven being weaving families.

In the other parts of Islington were 21 houses, of which only three had three storeys. Of this total, eleven were occupied by weaver householders, nine of them being weaving families.

THE DOWN

The Down – terraces on the east side (below left) and west side (above)

Beyond Islington, The Down consisted of three terraces of two-storeyed stone houses, built in the 1820s and 30s. These are still standing. In 1841 12 out of 24 households were headed by weavers, and eight of these were weaving families.

Adjoining The Down was Coal Ash Walk, which we now call Canal Road. Numbers 1, 3 and 5 are of the same type as those in The Down. In 1861 two of them were occupied by weavers, and the third was unoccupied except as a workshop. In 1870 they were for sale; the first had a front room, a kitchen, two bedrooms, and a weaving shop for four narrow looms 24 by 9 ft, the second had no weaving shop, and the third was similar to the first, the workshop 22 by 11 ft.

At this point we can make a comparison: in the Timbrell Street complex of streets there were 213 households, of which 29 were headed by weavers; about 73 houses here were of the top-floor workshop type, occupied at the most by 25 weaver householders – that is, if all the weaver householders on the east side of Timbrell Street and in Thomas Street lived in that type of house. In Islington and The Down there were 60 households, of which 32 were headed by weavers, virtually all in two-storeyed houses.

From this we can conclude that at this end of the town more weavers lived in houses of cottage type than in those with top-floor workshops.

THE CASTLE STREET – COURT STREET AREA

This is another part of the town which contained a proportion of houses with top-floor workshops. Here we still have well-preserved groups of five at the corner of Castle Street and Court Street, and seven on the east side of Castle Street. Six more on that side of the street have gone. On the west side of Castle Street a group of four stood at the corner with Mill Street, and nearby were Stainer's Buildings, a stone-built group of twelve. Elsewhere in the area was a group of four near the Bethesda Church in Court Street. Intermixed with these were many two-storeyed houses in other parts of Castle Street and Court Street and in St. Stephen's Place.

The corner of Castle Street and Court Street. This group was built in 1797.

Two pictures of the east side of Castle Street, taken from the corner of Mill Street, about forty years apart. The houses nearest the camera have gone but the upper part of the road remains. In 1841, no weavers lived on this side of the road despite the three storey houses.

The lower end of the east side of Castle Street in the 1950s. These houses were built in the 1820s and have now all gone.

The lower end of the west side of Castle Street. The pub to the left is the Elephant and Castle, now demolished like the rest of this group.

Stainer's Buildings ran at right angles to Castle Street through to Court Street. They first appear in the Trowbridge rate books in 1829. They were demolished in the early 1970s.

The only known surviving pictures of numbers 4 to 7 Court Street. The photographs can be dated to before 1931 because the factory lost its fifth floor in a fire in that year.

The 1841 census designates the whole of this simply as The Courts. In it were only seven weaver households all told, and four of these can be firmly located in courts behind the houses in the upper part of Castle Street; it is likely that courts behind streets only ever contained two-storey houses.

Another was in a two-storeyed house near the corner of St. Stephen's Place. One weaver, 72-year-old Daniel Rutter, lived in the house with a top-floor workshop indicated on the picture. This may well have been the only house of that type occupied by a weaver in the whole area.

In the Courts in 1841, of 38 houses with top-floor workshops only one was occupied by a weaver.

MORTIMER STREET AND NEW ROAD

Mortimer Street looking towards the town, 1905

Mortimer Street from the entrance to Longfield House. The only three-storeyed groups of houses are on the right.

The houses at the top of the south side of Mortimer Street had gardens in front.

Number 100 Mortimer Street from the front during demolition in the 1960s.

Apart from two houses with top-floor workshops near the corner of what became Bythesea Road, and one in New Road, still standing in the remaining fragment, this complex consisted entirely of two-storeyed houses, a considerable number in courts. In 1841 it contained 46 households headed by weavers, 16 of them being weaving families.

Even if the only three recorded houses with top-floor workshops in this area were weaver-occupied, 43 households headed by weavers were in two-storey buildings.

Workshop behind 5, New Road.

During demolitions in the 1960s Ken was able to photograph two apparent weaving shops behind houses. Unfortunately, neither can be firmly associated with weaver occupiers. The left hand one was behind No. 100 Mortimer Street and was probably the former weaving shop 20 by 11 ft with two bedrooms over in this part of the street advertised in 1874. The right hand one was behind No. 5 New Road. In the photograph it can be seen that the upper part of the blank wall facing the camera had been rebuilt, suggesting that there was originally a long window there. The workshop behind No. 100 Mortimer Street, the house of William Deverall, book keeper, is mentioned below.

NEWTOWN still has a row of three-storeyed houses, some in original states. They were begun in 1790.

Numbers 14 to 17 Newtown.

Numbers 18 to 22 Newtown

There was another row on the same side of the road towards Trinity Church. In it were probably eight houses on the street, some back to back. Behind both rows were courts.

This glimpse of the backs of those nearest Gloucester Road suggest that they were of three storeys

We can begin with the latter, now disappeared. In 1841 there were about 45 households so there must have been some multiple occupation. Of these, 17 were headed by weavers, ten of them weaving families. When one of the three-storeyed houses in this part was for sale in 1867, all the upper rooms were in use as bedrooms, but there was a workshop on two floors adjoining.

In the preserved part, we can for once be specific to some extent. We use today's numbers.

No. 14: 1841, 1851, 1861 beer house.
No. 15: 1841, weaver with wife and daughter; 1851 and 1861, slaymaker.
No. 16: 1841, shearman, wife and two others weavers; 1851, handloom weaver and wife; 1861, coach builder, sister-in-law weaver.
No. 17: 1841, weaver; 1851 and 1861, market gardener.
No. 18: 1841, cloth dresser, wife weaver; 1851, weaver; 1861, carpenter.
No. 19: 1841, weaver with son, daughter-in-law, and daughter; 1851, brush maker; 1861, carpenter.
No. 20: 1841, spinner, wife weaver; 1851, factory overlooker, wife handloom weaver; 1861, weaver with a lodger.
No. 21: 1841, clerk; 1851 (same man), house agent; 1861, iron moulder.

No. 22: 1841, vacant; 1851, book keeper, wife weaver; 1861 (same man), weaver.

No. 23: 1841, three households, two of them weavers; 1851, handloom weaver with wife and daughter; 1861, weaver with wife and two daughters.

No. 24: 1841, teazle planter, wife and one other weavers; 1851 (same man), farmer, wife weaver; 1861, (same man), agricultural labourer (but in fact a teazle grower and merchant whose account book survives).

No. 25: 1841, butcher; 1851 clothworker; 1861, servant.

No. 26: 1841, butcher and clothier; 1851, spinner; 1861, spinner, wife weaver.

No. 27: 1841 weaver; 1851 (same man), weaver; 1861, weaver with wife.

After number 27 Newtown, it is more difficult to be certain of the identity of individual properties, as there were courts of houses behind the street nearer to Wesley Road. Within this area, in 1841 there were four more weaver households. In 1851 there were five more weaver households. In 1861 there were two more weaver households and three other weavers.

In Newtown, therefore, we can at least say that the top-floor workshop type of house was more likely to be used by a resident weaver than in the other groups so far considered. We can consider some other groups of this type more briefly.

BRADFORD ROAD
(formerly
TROWLE LANE)

There were several three-storey houses in a row on the northeast side. They had gone by the mid 1960s. No weavers in the street in 1841.

YERBURY STREET

The houses nearest the camera were built in 1793. The further two houses were added in 1818.

The two classic examples of this type at the end of the street.

No weaver household in the street in 1841, only one wife and one lodger.

NAISH'S YARD, HILL STREET
Naish's Yard had a complex history and is discussed later in this book. There were seven weaver households in Naish's Yard in 1841, three of them families.

POLEBARN BUILDINGS

This was a group of eight three-storeyed houses built back-to-back at the bottom of Polebarn Road south of the way into Ashton Street. There was one weaver in this part of the street in 1841; the group can be identified in 1851, but with no weavers. These lasted until about 1980.

DURSLEY ROAD

There were a group of three three-storeyed houses at the junction with Mortimer Street, occupied by four weaving families and one weaver in 1841. In the one nearest the camera in the lower picture lived Daniel Lucas who took part in the 1863 controversy discussed later. These were demolished in the 1950s.

THE BRICK PLAT

Three ranks of houses, called collectively the Brick Plat, running off the northwest side of Union Street, had origins in the mid-18th century. Two ranks disappeared early in the twentieth century unrecorded, but the third survived until the 1960s. It consisted of three-storeyed houses, evidently built to provide working space.

There were twelve weaver households in the Brick Plat in 1841. One weaver, who certainly lived in the row shown, was Roger Brown, father of

Samuel and grandfather of William Roger, who both became very wealthy manufacturers in the town.

St Thomas's Passage, Brick Plat

The rear view of St Thomas's Terrace (above and above right) suggests that industrial processes may have been carried out on the ground floor

Number 15, St Thomas's Passage. The upper floor appears to have been added to an earlier building, perhaps when top floor workshops became common. Thomas Richmond, broad and narrow weaver, who gave evidence to the Parliamentary Enquiry of 1802-3, lived here.

No. 15 was originally two houses, owned at his death in 1778 by the Trowbridge architect Esau Reynolds. In 1802 they were bought by Thomas Richmond, weaver, who converted them into one for his own occupation. Judging by the size, he must have been a master weaver employing several looms.

Included here because the picture does not fit neatly anywhere else, this house in Church Street was built about 1690 but had a second floor with weaver's windows added much later. No weavers lived in Church Street in 1841.

STUDLEY FIELDS

This pair of three-storey houses were the only ones in what was then a rural location. They now stand in Cherry Gardens and bear the initials of James Bodman and the date 1798. Bodman, who was a small clothier, lived in an adjoining house. He subsequently wrote a history of Trowbridge published in 1814. Both were occupied by weavers in 1841.

From these scattered examples we get the same impression, that only a moderate proportion of houses with the extra facility of a third, workshop, floor were occupied by weavers. There were, of course, other cloth trade purposes for which such shops could be used. One was jenny spinning. Arthur Perkins Stancomb said that when he entered the trade in 1841 many jennies were used in cottages. In 1863 a house to let in Hilperton Road had room for two jennies and reels. The large and well-equipped firm of Brown and Palmer was having spinning done at home in 1866. Burling was another process carried on domestically. As late as 1870 a house in The Conigre with rooms suitable for burling was advertised. Some cloth working by hand survived until the 1840s, and might have been done domestically for small clothiers. In 1862 John Dicks of Stallard Street was in his workshop at the top of the house when a bullet came through the window; it would have killed his son if he had been at work in his usual place. The report describes him as a clothworker, though he appears in the census as a grocer!

Though not strictly relevant, we must include a report of an inquest in 1869 on the wife of a weaver named Arnold, who lived in Newtown. He went downstairs early in the morning and had just woven one quill when he heard what he thought was two cats quarrelling in the next room. Not finding any cats there, the thought struck him that it must be Hannah a-dying, and sure enough it was....

THE TOWN CENTRE

Many other weaver householders appear in the 1841 census in the inner area of the town, but in parts such as The Conigre, Shails Lane and Frog Lane, where it is not possible to locate them exactly enough to comment on their accommodation. In those three locations there were 36 weaver householders in 1841, but only four of them wove with other members of their families. This suggests at least the possibility that weavers living in the town itself were more likely to work in the weaving shops which we know were at or used in conjunction with some of the factories.

The Conigre consisted originally of two-storeyed houses built in the late 17th and early 18th centuries. Pictures taken during the demolition in 1935 suggest that at least some had had third storeys added.

A house in Lower Broad Street, Conigre, which is known to have been owned and occupied by weavers named Long for many years after Charles

Long bought it in 1808, had, when it was for sale in 1873, on the ground floor a parlour and a kitchen and weaving shop 23 by 11 ft, and a bedroom or weaving shop of the same size over. A master weaver with this much space may well have employed weavers who lived in their own houses.

Trowbridge's best example of a weaver's window was in the road called The Conigre. As with other houses in the vicinity, the second floor has been added at a later date. Conigre Parsonage, which still survives, can be seen at the left of the lower photograph.

The only four-storeyed group in Trowbridge was Nos. 6, 7, and 8 in Back Street. The nearby Conigre Church owned three ruinous houses on the site, and in 1800 made a lease to the clothier Francis Naish on condition that he built three houses. After he moved to Twerton in 1804 they were put up for sale, occupied by James Pitman, later a weaver in Timbrell Street, and others. Between 1821 and 1841 one was occupied by James Sims, a spinner, and another spinner, John Lintern, was in another of the houses from 1835 to 1841. It seems likely that this group was of the type that combined workshop and domestic accommodation, of which I described examples in Yerbury Street and Duke Street (Nos. 4 and 22) in my *Clothiers' Workshops*.

Outside the area of the town as it was in 1841, there were only two three-storeyed houses (at Studley Fields, as discussed above), and so we can be reasonably confident that in these areas the vast majority of weavers lived and worked in two-storey buildings.

The table below shows weavers in the outer parts of the parish in 1841.

Area	*Householders*	*Of which families*
Lower Studley	36	28
Middle Studley	20	17
Silver Street Lane	8	8
Studley Green	20	7
Whiterow	12	5

Of the weaving families, the largest was that of James Davis in Dursley Lane who in 1851 had a wife and five children from 18 to 27.

STAVERTON AND OVER THE PARISH BOUNDARY

STAVERTON WAS ACTUALLY part of Trowbridge parish but was a separate chapelry and we have treated it separately for the purposes of this book.

This group stood in Staverton but cannot be identified in 1841. The arrangement of the chimneys suggests that they were back to back houses.

Over the parish boundary the same concentration of weavers continued in what had by then become North Bradley parish, which then included Southwick and the Wiltshire part of Rode. In 1841, for instance, there were weaver households in that parish in places as follows:

Area	Weaving households
Yarnbrook	17
Little Common	11
Drynham	4
Woodmarsh	9
The Rank	20
Axe and Cleaver	5
Kingsbridge	2
Bradley	15
Parsons Corner	7
Ireland	7
Brokerswood	5
Poleshole	19

Hoopers Pool	2
Bradley Common	1
Furze Knap	1
Southwick	22
Warp Lane	11
Parish Road	5
Rode Common	9
Rode	7
Hilperton Marsh	9
Total	187

OTHER TOWNS

ONE EXAMPLE OF the 'Trowbridge type' of three-storeyed weavers house is shown in this view (opposite) of St Margaret's Passage, Bradford.

A distinctive type of weaver's house not known in Trowbridge appears in Bradford, with a three light window to one side of the door which was the weaving shop and a two light window to the other which was the kitchen.

The groups on the Trowbridge Road in Bradford were advertised in 1823 as fifteen new-built weavers' houses in two rows. Each contains a shop for two broadlooms, a kitchen and three bedrooms, with a brewhouse and garden behind.

Other examples of this type can be seen in Regent Place, Bradford and in Dymott Square in Hilperton.

Several terraces of three-storeyed houses still exist in Frome and others have not survived. However, Frome would merit a separate book and awaits investigation. The same is true of a group at Chippenham. No houses of the type under discussion are known by us to have existed in Westbury, Warminster or Melksham.

We should also note here that some three-storeyed groups, such as Weaver's Cottages (formerly Factory Row) at Seend and groups on The Green at Calne were actually built as clothiers machinery workshops and were only converted to houses when that use ceased.

It is clear, then, that the great majority of weavers in Trowbridge and the surrounding villages in 1841, before the introduction of the power loom locally, did not live in three-storey houses, contrary to conventional belief.

SHOP WEAVING

By 1700 the great majority of cloths made in our area were medleys – made of short-staple wool, first dyed then prepared for spinning by scribbling, woven broad, fulled at the mill, and finished by lengthy and skilled cloth working. Scribbling made it possible to mix dyed wools of different colours to produce cloths of a variety of colours, but without pattern or visible weave. We should regard them as heavy, about like what would be used for an overcoat today. They were sometimes known as Spanish cloths from the imported merino wool, but only the most expensive cloths used it entirely; for cheaper grades it would be mixed with good quality English wool in varying proportions. Even these were a luxury product, a yard often costing more than the people making them could earn in a week.

Weaving such cloths had to be carefully done but was not of a complicated nature. As we have seen this was undertaken entirely by cottage weavers but this changed with the introduction of the fancy trade, as we shall see.

Defoe's enthusiastic description of this trade is well-known – 'the finest Spanish medley cloths, not in England only, but in the whole world, are made in this part.' He picked out Bradford and Trowbridge as the two most eminent towns, and it seems clear that they were at the apex of the trade. Trowbridge and Bradford cloths were mentioned in a broadside of 1713 as though they were a recognised product. The London factor James Elderton, remonstrating with one of his clothiers for expecting too high a price in 1768, pointed out (in the same letter) that 'the very best cloths that are made in England will fetch no more than 16s. a yard … the very best that are made at Bradford and Trowbridge will sell for no more than 16s.'

CASSIMERES AND THE FANCY TRADE

At the very time when Elderton wrote these words, a new element was coming into this well-established industry.

Cassimere was a type of cloth patented by the Bradford clothier Francis Yerbury in 1766. Yerbury described it as 'a new manner of making thin superfine cloth for the summer season at home and warmer climates abroad, yet notwithstanding the thinness of its texture it is more durable than cloth of a greater substance made in the common way'.

The impact of Yerbury's patent was immediate. In 1769 a shop in Bath advertised 'kerzey-meere' coats. In 1770 John Cook of Trowbridge, baker, and James Little of Bradford, weaver, entered into a partnership to practice 'the art, mystery, or trade of making and manufacturing a sort of woollen cloth called or known by the name of casimeres, being a manufacture differing from all sorts and kinds of other woollen goods'. The Salisbury drapers Ogden and Hillman advertised cassimeres among cloths that they sold in 1770.

In 1771 ten looms of the sort required for weaving cassimeres were for sale at Chippenham; they had been in use for three years. White cassimere cloth was stolen from a rack in Trowbridge in 1773. In 1775 a Salisbury draper advertised superfine cassimeres at 6s a yard and scarlet ones at 7s; he also had 'exceeding fine thin cloths for ladies riding dresses'. Sixteen cassimere looms were for sale at Bradford in 1776.

Bailey's Directory of 1783 reveals how the trade had developed a whole new sector. Most clothiers still described themselves as manufacturers of superfines, seconds, or liveries, but some had gone into the new trade:

Bradford	John Yerbury, clothier and cassameer manufacturer
Chippenham	Richard Singer and Co. manufacturers of superfine cloth and cassameers
Melksham	Joseph Yerbury, clothier and manufacturer of ladies cloths and cassimeres
Salisbury	William Jesser, fancy cloth manufacturer Henry Wansey, manufacturer of flannels, linseys, cottons, and also yard wide fancy cloths
Trowbridge	John Clark, manufacturer of cassimeers [Not the man of this name who was also a minister.] James Coles, manufacturer of ladies cloths, cassimeers, and fancy cloths Samuel Cook, manufacturer of fancy and superfine cloths Nicholas and John Cross, manufacturers of superfine cloths and cassimeres Edward Horlock Mortimer, manufacturer of ladies cloths, cassimeers, and all fancy cloths James Selfe, superfine clothier and manufacturer of ladies cloths and cassimeres John and Thomas Stillman, superfine and ladies cloth manufacturers
Frome	William and Walter Sheppard, superfine clothier and cassimeer manufacturer.

There may, of course, have been other people in this trade who did not specify it to the compilers of the directory. It is to be noted, for instance, that John Anstie of Devizes, the largest of all the fancy manufacturers, appears simply as clothier.

In 1784 an advertisement in the *Salisbury Journal* wanted 'a sober careful man to superintend a small manufactory. One who is a complete master of the business in the plain and fancy way will meet with the greatest encouragement.' In 1785 Samuel Cook of Trowbridge was using silk yarn in his cloths; we know this because 'a fugitive and pilfering weaver' went off leaving his work unfinished and took some of the yarn with him. Cook still had some silk when his goods were sold on his bankruptcy in 1804.

It is unfortunate that whereas pattern books of clothiers in the broadcloth trade survive in some numbers, we have few patterns to illustrate the designs which must have led to the designation 'fancy'. Francis Yerbury's own pattern book, inexplicably surviving among the records of Salters of Trowbridge, contains almost entirely single colour cassimeres; only at the end are a few simple striped pieces. Another book (WSHC 719/1) of an unnamed clothier, almost certainly from Trowbridge, 1774-85, includes only a few cassimeres towards the end, one with a herringbone pattern. But no surviving pattern is of anything like the complexity of two pieces of narrow cloth which were stolen from the tenters of John Yerbury, Francis's son and successor, in 1778. 'One strip'd with a narrow pink stripe between two white ones, on a sage green ground on which was black and buff spots. One a broad pearl coloured stripe on which is green and white spots and a lead coloured stripe with orange and white spots and a narrow white stripe between the two'.

Here we have an immediate contrast with the weaving required to produce broadcloth, which was of the simplest kind. All the art of making good broadcloth lay in the other processes – thorough scribbling to mix the colours, fine spinning, and skilful cloth working. Nor was the weaving of plain cassimeres much more complex; the 2/2 twill which produced the ribbed surface only requires four harnesses on the loom. The use of a draw loom, in which a 'draw boy' assisted the weaver by raising and lowering the harnesses, was unknown in our area, so the only way to weave a complex pattern was to use a loom with many treadles, each attached to one harness. A visitor to Palmer and Mackay's factory in the early 20th century was shown a handloom which had 16 treadles, believed to be much more than a hundred years old. Rees's *Cyclopaedia* points out the difficulty of using a loom like this: 'The number of treadles requisite to raise all the heddles which must be used to produce very extensive patterns, would be more than one man could manage;

for if he placed his foot by mistake on a wrong treadle he would disfigure his pattern.'

The introduction of fancy cloths made it necessary to carry out the more complex weaving required in workshops under the master's supervision. Apart from William Stump's apparently short-lived attempt to introduce it in the 16th century, when he filled the former Malmesbury Abbey buildings with looms, there is no indication of weaving being done elsewhere than in the weavers' premises until the introduction of fancy cloths made it necessary. Two of the clothiers mentioned in the 1783 directory clearly had looms in their own workshops – William Jesser had ten looms at his death in 1784, and Richard Singer of Chippenham had 23 kerseymere looms when his goods were sold after his death in 1803. William Sheppard of Frome summed it up in 1803, saying 'It is necessary to work under the master's eye in fancy work, or they would be perpetually making blunders. On plain work, such as broad cloth and cassimere, no evil is to be apprehended.'

John Anstie's workshop in New Park Street, Devizes

One weaving shop on a large scale is that still standing in New Park Street, Devizes, which bears the initials of John Anstie and the date 1785. This was before the introduction of either carding or spinning machinery and makes it clear that it was certainly built for weaving. It was remembered in 1803 as 'a weaving factory in a borough town'. Anstie told a contemporary that he employed 300 looms; he was chosen to chair the meetings described below because he made almost entirely fancy cassimeres.

John Waldon of Trowbridge is mentioned simply as a clothier in 1783. The following year he built the fine house now called Westcroft in British Row, and this building a short distance away at about the same time. It passed with the Waldon business to John Henry Webb, who was using it for jenny spinning in the middle of the nineteenth century. It seems a reasonable guess that it was built for a weaving shop.

It has not been possible to identify the location of any other workshops in this trade, in Trowbridge or elsewhere, with any certainty.. On the premises of James Selfe was a building, the town rate of which was as high as some of smaller factories which appeared later. It adjoined Rodney House, where Selfe lived, and was said to be little used by 1808. Cook had large premises in Duke Street which later formed part of a factory. These could well have included space for fancy weaving.

OPPOSITION TO SHOP WEAVING

IT SEEMS TO have been shop weaving that led to disturbances at Trowbridge early in 1787. On 2 January 'a very formidable mob of weavers assembled together, in consequence of lately feeling an infringement of their rights from a certain clothier of the town; after remonstrating in a sensible manner ... and at the same time threatening to the terror of many of the first order of clothiers present, that if they had not immediate assurances of a firm and full restoration of their rights, they were resolved on a demolition of shops...'. A clothier assured them, on behalf of his brethren, that their requisition would be complied with. 'Thus ended an affair that made stout men tremble in their shoes'.

The next week a letter to the paper from A.B. of Trowbridge said that the matter had been entirely misreported; the weavers had simply been told wrongly that a lowering of the price of their work was intended. The clothiers assured them that this was not so, and threatened stern measures unless they dispersed, which they immediately did.

Late in January a mob of broad and narrow weavers and others, said to number 1,500, mostly armed with clubs and other weapons, assembled by appointment at Trowbridge, and forced the clothiers to agree to their demands. They then went to Bradford, where they were forced to retreat by the gentlemen, assisted by a large number of special constables. Their final target was Mr Yerbury's house at Belcombe Brook; he had placed two 'pateraroes' [a type of small cannon] in his parlour windows, and was supported by many well-armed friends. The mob then dispersed, and the military arrived the next day.

On 17 February a meeting was held at Trowbridge between the local Justices, the cassimere makers, and representatives appointed by different districts to present the complaints of the weavers. After much deliberation, the Justices recommended that the clothiers should give up weaving plain cassimeres in their shops, but agreed that it was necessary that fancy cassimeres should continue to be woven in the shops. Some of the clothiers who had shops 'represented in forcible terms' the disadvantages which would arise from giving them up, and the Justices admitted that, though they wished for a compromise, there was nothing illegal in their having them, and they would be bound to protect their persons and property. The meeting then continued with the presentation of several calculations advanced by each side of what the weavers could earn, which the chairman thought were erroneous – so the dispute was at least partly about earnings. In the end the weavers were sent away with only a reiteration of the Justices' position.

They left the meeting promising to be guilty of no disorders, yet on 20 February another meeting at Trowbridge had to be broken up by the reading of the Riot Act and the intervention of the military; several rioters were wounded and four arrested. John Abbott of Melksham and George Gardener of North Bradley were later sent to prison for three years, and James Cogswell of Trowbridge for one year. The Salisbury paper commented on their good fortune in escaping the ignominious death which would have been:

the just reward for their temerity, which they may attribute wholly to the lenity of their prosecutors, and the clemency of their judge. His lordship in his charge, animadverted very ably on the evil tendency of their crime, which he said was of the most daring and malignant nature, committed in the very face and in defiance of the civil and military power, replete with the most alarming consequence to society, and particularly to the interests of this country, as tending to a general subversion, if not a total annihilation of trade, and therefore deserving of the most exemplary punishment. His lordship also made some severe remarks on the conduct of a certain gentleman in that neighbourhood, who had been active in encouraging the rioters, and observed, that though he was not a defendant in this indictment, yet if his conduct was such as it had been represented to be, he was liable to be called to an account for it at that bar, or in the Ecclesiastical Court.

We can make no guess about who this last sentence refers to. Could this have been a local clergyman?

Bath Chronicle 1st March 1787
To the printer of the Bath Chronicle
Sir I beg to leave the following positions to the public which are founded on the strictest truth. That the weavers having for some time part past threatened the clothiers of Trowbridge were their intention of pulling down the shops erected for the purposes of weaving cassimere in their own houses at last assembled in a very large body and entering the town compelled the clothiers by force and violence the promise that their shop should be discontinued. That the time when these outrages were committed it does not appear that the narrow weavers were unemployed but on the contrary that the numbers of looms employed by the weavers themselves in their own houses had increased. That having attended the first meeting at Trowbridge at the request of a gentleman from Melksham and one from Chippenham whom I met at the House of a worthy magistrate and who also wished me to be present I'm being unanimously decided to act as chairman the first object of my inquiry was whether the promises given by the clothiers to the weavers were voluntary as in this case my principals would not me permit me to interfere. That every person declared it was merely from fear of injury to their persons and properties that they gave the promises to the weavers which agreeable to the most established principles of morals are in such cases not binding but fully justifies the resolution of the glove is to this effect. That the poor proposition weaving claimed plane Kassam ears at 10 pence per yard instead of 11 pence were originally from some of the weavers

themselves and can come be considered in the light other than in no other light Sanderson motor settlement which may induce the clothiers not only to forebear erecting more shops but they also tend to decrease those which are now existing. That the weavers absolutely rejected the propositions of the manufacturers when present at the meeting of the justices those strongly recommended to accept them by the magistrates and continued to manifest a determination of opposing those persons who kept shops which rendered it absolutely necessary to suspend the trade though it would unavoidably bring distress on some innocent persons. That the present rate of wages in the shops is in general higher than is given by the master weavers to their journeyman as it came out at the meeting of the justices there in some parts of the country the master weavers had much oppressed their journey man by obliging them through necessity to work for very low wages. That it is unjust to assert that the clothing is wish to reduce the price of weaving simply considered but On the contrary it can be viewed in no other light than as a mutual compact to give up one advantage in order to procure another. If ever there was a moment when the manufacturers ought to act in concert it is the present one I can safely trust to my general character as guarding me from the imputation of oppressing the poor and I'm confident that the man who with a firm temperate conduct opposes the illegal attempts of the Workman is most essentially their friend the part which I've taken in this business is grounded simply on a determined resolution not to submit to the menaces of a mob and this resolution has been amply manifested in my conduct towards my own men. The feelings of my mind would be more gratified by adhering simply to a general and determined opposition of every combination amongst Workman to coerce manufacturers without catering entering into any agreement whatsoever but my single opinion will always bend to the wish of the general body when I am convinced that there is no injustice in their conduct. The questions have been asked me concerning the present subject and the desire of not appearing to countenance oppression must be my apology for the publication of these observations. I am and Co J Anstey. Devizes February the 28th.

Another meeting was held in Bath on 7 March, attended by cassimere makers from Devizes, Trowbridge, Melksham, Frome, Rode, Chippenham, and Bromham. They began by stating that the advantages of shop weaving to the clothiers were so great, 'though by no means agreeable to many of the manufacturers' [apparently here meaning weavers, though meaning clothiers elsewhere in the account], that it was likely to become universal unless a method could be found of 'equalizing the advantages between the manufacturers in point of weaving'. Prices were set at eightpence a yard for shop woven cassimeres and tenpence a yard for those put out, the weavers of the latter finding their own tackling. Many of the manufacturers declared their intention of not weaving plain cassimeres at home (that is in a shop), and several others who had intended to erect shops were now happy to let the weavers have the looms in their own houses. This seems to have satisfied the weavers, and shop weaving for fancy goods continued.

> *Speedily will be published, addressed to the Gentlemen of Landed Property in the county of Wilts,*
>
> A Particular Account of the Dispute which has lately taken place between the Clothiers of Trowbridge and their Weavers; together with some account of the proceedings at Trowbridge on the 26th of February last. To which is added, a short Sketch of the Evidence produced in Court on the part of the prosecution at the trial of George Gardiner, Abbot, Outley, and Cogfal, at the assizes in Sarum, on Wednesday the 14th day of March 1787; together with the Evidence ready to be produced on the part of the Defendants, had the Counsel for the Defendants thought proper to have brought it forward.
>
> The character of the Vicar of North-Bradley having been reflected upon in public court, renders the above publication necessary.
>
> By the Rev. CHARLES DAUBENY, LL. B.
> Vicar of North-Bradley, Fellow of Winchester college, and Prebendary of Sarum. [8-7-]

An advertisement in the Bath Chronicle of 22 March 1787. No copy of the pamphlet is known to exist.

CHANGES OF FORTUNE IN THE FANCY TRADE

IT SEEMS LIKELY that the local manufacture of fancy cassimeres declined in the 1790s. Lorna Haycock in her *John Anstie of Devizes* quotes sources showing the extent of his trade with the continent, and especially 'the avidity with which the French purchase our fancy goods'. He was making mixtures of wool mixed with silk in stripes, checks, and spotted and figured cloths, the stripes selling particularly well in Russia. Even Marie Antoinette chose one of his patterns. Mrs Haycock discusses several factors leading to his bankruptcy in 1793; it seems likely that an important one must have been the cutting off of this continental trade following the outbreak of war with France.

It may have been the same difficulty that led an unnamed Trowbridge clothier to give up in 1791, leaving 90 superfine cloths and cassimeres in different stages of manufacture to be sold. John Cook, whose weaving 'factory' with twenty looms was remembered by a witness in the 1803 Parliamentary Report on the State of the Woollen Industry, gave up in 1794. The advertisement of his premises in Duke Street mentions 'every conveniency for the residence of the workpeople employed therein', as though he had some of them living in; he also had 'some excellent tenements, built purposely for the accommodation of the manufacturers engaged in any part of the business'.

Some records of the firm Hanson and Mills, Blackwell factors, are now in the National Archives (C 113/18). Their stock book for 1795 shows cloths held for a number of local clothiers, but categorizes them simply as cassimeres or cloths. The Trowbridge firm of N. and J. Cross also supplied swansdowns, a cheaper cloth.

There is also a letter book, from which we can tell that some of the cassimeres were piece dyed – for example, John Clark of Trowbridge, 1795, 'not dyed to pattern'; Mr Deane of Trowbridge, to supply 'a few ends of superfine dyed cloths for the Russian trade'; William Phelps of Bradford for superfine blacks. Hanson and Mills also pointed out to John Clark of Trowbridge in 1795 that breeches of cassimere were now worn of the same colour as the coat; he should therefore see what was being made in cloth coatings and make his cassimeres of the same colours, drab colours being much wanted.

John Wilshire of Melksham made the cheap cloths called Plunketts; Hanson and Mills had lost their foreign buyers for these on account of the inferior quality of Wilshire's cloth – 'colours too dark and dye rubs off it and shows white patches. Some Yorkshire ones sent out by the same vessel were worth much more on account of their superior colour'.

I have mentioned the Hanson and Mills records at length to show that, as far as can be told, none of the goods that they handled for local clothiers required anything in the nature of fancy weaving. The records also include a pattern book which Roy Berrett, the last general manager of Salter's in Trowbridge, has examined and has kindly passed us what he has discovered.

There are, firstly, some striped cloth, produced simply by inserting the appropriate coloured yarn for the stripes in the warp so that the stripes run lengthways on the cloth. This requires no more than normal weaving once the loom is set up. Some other patterns in the book came as a surprise to Roy and to me. They are of cassimeres with elaborate patterns produced by block printing. The factors presumably had this done in London, and the clothier simply supplied pieces of the required base colour, so again no more than plain weaving is required. Whether this became a regular practice and for how long it lasted is at present quite unknown. Records of retailers of cloth would be needed to discover this.

So, the Hanson and Mills records show little or no sign of fancy weaving. On the other hand, Francis Naish of Trowbridge advertised in 1791 for twenty narrow weavers to work in shops on cassimeres, silk, and fancy cloths, and in 1793 a Horningsham clothier wanted a man to overlook a woollen manufacture who had been accustomed to make cassimeres and fancy cloth. Naish's trade was in making fancy patterns for waistcoats and he and his father before him occupied a complex of buildings at the bottom of Wicker Hill on the later site of Bridge Mill. We have a detailed description of these from an insurance policy of 1805 which shows that they included a weaving shop.

It seems likely that Naish's attempt to get local weavers to work in shop had not proved successful, for in 1794 he advertised 'Wanted immediately from twenty to thirty narrow weavers who have been used to weave silk, fancy woollens, worsted or tick. Good and useful hands, who follow their work will meet with constant employ and good wages by applying at Mr Naish's Manufactory, Trowbridge'.

Now this advertisement appeared in the *Sherborne Mercury*, a newspaper little known in West Wiltshire, but likely to be seen in the Mere area, where there was an extensive tick manufacture, or south-east Somerset where there was some silk industry. So it looks as though Naish was finding difficulty in overcoming the prejudice of local weavers against working in shop and was desperate to get any who would do so. We can go further. In 1793 Naish had bought from a shopkeeper, Benjamin Cogswell, a court of houses running back from Hill Street in Trowbridge. Later rating records show them as houses with three long rooms over them. This suggests an arrangement little known in our area, although common in some textile districts, of having upper rooms running over several houses. It is probable that the 44 looms which Naish had in 1803, (in a report described below), were here. The only other local example known to us of an arrangement of this kind are houses that formerly stood in the location of the High Street in Westbury.

Houses at Westbury on the site of the present day High Street car park. The top floor ran the whole length of the building without partitions.

By 1801 Naish had expanded enormously. At the peace celebrations in 1801 he provided an excellent dinner to upwards of 500 of his workpeople.

Naish was a particular target of the shearmen in the disturbances of 1802. He owned the mill at Littleton, burnt down by the party which included Thomas Hilliker who was subsequently hanged at Salisbury. It was let to Ralph Heath, who said in his evidence at Hilliker's trial that he used it for fulling and spinning, but it seems likely that he must have been using, or that he was believed to be using, the hated finishing machinery.

Other workshops in the Conigre in Trowbridge belonging to Naish were also destroyed; these may have been used for machinery. Almost immediately the large factory at Twerton was advertised for sale and he moved his trade there, where he had extensive weaving shops and continued to manufacture fancy goods.

Naish was clearly in the fancy trade, as his subsequent career shows. He apparently survived two more bankruptcies and took out a patent for silk mixed with other articles. When he went bankrupt at Twerton in 1817 he was using 40 broad and 120 narrow spring looms. This was the name used in the west for looms with a fly shuttle. Although we have no certain information, we think it quite possible that the row of houses now known as Rackfield Place in Twerton began as weaving workshops.

—Yesterday morning, the people employed at Mr Nash's, Twerton factory, entered the city in procession—men, women, and children, all dressed in their holiday attire, and preceded by a band of music, and displaying laurels, flags, ribbons &c. In the happy groupe was a car, on which a loom was placed, and a man and two children cheerfully at work—a pleasing emblem of the renovation of our manufacturing interests: the car was decked with mottos, appropriate to the inspiriting occasion, and the whole procession was hailed with reiterated shouts by the surrounding crowds. Madame Catalani, on their passing her hotel, sent 2 pounds to the festive party, to assist in their merry making.

From the Bristol Mirror 16 April 1814

Rackfield Place in Twerton

By the time of his death, aged 73, he was living at Glastonbury. His family advertised the patent for sale, together with a large stock of raw materials and machinery there.

There may also have been other fancy manufacturers in Trowbridge by the end of the eighteenth century. Cloths stolen from tenters on Court Hill in Trowbridge in 1799 included ladies cloth, a fancy weave.

The only fancy goods manufacturer mentioned in the 1805 directory was Robert Waylen of Devizes. His career, in which he occupied at different times Snake Mead mill, a steam driven factory in Northgate Street and the former Anstie workshops in New Park Street, is traced in *Wiltshire and Somerset Woollen Mills*. He was also in partnership with Peter Walker as a silk throwster. When he gave up clothing in 1821 he had five narrow looms, a thousand fancy and cassimere slays and harnesses and a hundred spring shuttles. A later reminiscence shows that he made fancy waistcoatings.

There had been an attempt to introduce spring looms to Trowbridge in 1792 which had resulted in violent opposition and evidently a withdrawal of their use, as described in this extract from the *Bath Chronicle* of that year.

> The Clothiers of Trowbridge last week entertained serious apprehensions of a riot among their workmen, who supposed themselves injured by the introduction of machines in the manufactory, to lessen the quantity of manual labour [spring looms] – the dragoons quartered at Bradford were on Thursday called in, with the aid of those quartered at Trowbridge; notwithstanding which, a very numerous mob assembled on Friday, and it was at length deemed advisable by one of the Magistrates to read the Riot Act, when they all dispersed, without committing any acts of violence; the alarm was however so great, that additional troops are already ordered to be quartered at Trowbridge and Bradford.

In 1803 a Parliamentary Committee was appointed to hear petitions submitted on behalf of workpeople to revive ancient statutes which might be held to prohibit the use of the gig mill, to require apprenticeship for weavers and to limit the number of looms any person could have. The 1803 Parliamentary enquiry provides an interesting picture of the local trade at that time.

As could be expected several clothiers said that the art of weaving could be acquired in about a year, whereas weavers suggested it required seven years. One enterprising weaver called Joseph Bailey from Rode actually took along a piece of fancy weaving and showed it to the Committee. The use of the spring loom and shop weaving were particularly sensitive to weavers locally.

The Report shows that spring looms were only in use in Wiltshire at Francis Hill's large factory at Malmesbury, where he had about sixty. A

Bradford weaver who gave evidence had gone to Malmesbury with his wife to weave in spring looms. They found it much harder work, and the wife could not stand it. The quality of the weaving was also very poor. Hill provided not only the looms but also size and glue, slay, and harnesses, the weaver supplying shuttle and bobbins.

The evidence of this couple illustrates one objection the domestic weavers had to shop weaving; the hours were fixed with no candle work, 7 ½ hours in winter rising to a maximum of 12 in the summer. At home they could work from 5 am to 7 pm in winter and from 4 pm to 9pm in summer. A North Bradley man said that the weavers would have to go several miles to work i.e. daily to shops in Trowbridge rather than once in three or four weeks to get a chain. Another point raised was the difficulty of training children to weave except in the home.

The report makes it clear that there were no weaving shops or spring looms in Wiltshire outside Malmesbury. It mentions that a weaver from North Bradley stated that he had never seen a spring loom. Thomas Joyce of Freshford told the enquiry that a clothier who had been in the north had tried to introduce spring looms about two years before, but had had to abandon them after a few weeks because of riotous opposition. Miss Mann, in her *The Woollen Industry in the West of England from 1640 to 1880* (p. 141) assumed that this was at Freshford, but it may have been at Chippenham, where there was rioting at that time. And weaving shops were mentioned only in the recent past – Anstie at Devizes, Cook and Naish at Trowbridge, and a 'cassimere factory' (no doubt Singer's) in Chippenham. John Jones of Staverton Factory said that he was not aware of weavers being forced to work in shops; he employed 90 broad [domestic] looms – to have 100 at the factory he would need a building 100 feet by 35 feet of four storeys, which would cost two or three thousand pounds.

William Sheppard of Frome went even further – 'no manufacturer will find it worth his while to erect such immense work, a quarter-or a half-mile long'.

The Wiltshire situation was in great contrast to that in Gloucestershire, where the spring loom was in widespread use. The clothiers there had no complaints about the quality of the weaving; the advantage was to the weaver, in that it was faster; the work was harder, but could be done by a healthy woman. There was some shop weaving, but it was not liked by the clothiers on grounds of the expense of building the shops, and the time taken to supervise the work. Daniel Lloyd of Uley said that he was the first to introduce cassimeres into that neighbourhood and that when he began, he was obliged to have his weavers on his premises to teach them. He once had 50 or 60 looms, 'but as fast as we had weavers to take them away that understood it, we let them go; we have now about twelve, which we should be happy to part with, if we could get honest weavers to take them; we want the room very much for other things'. Edward Sheppard, also of Uley, said that Gloucestershire had gained much of this trade from Wiltshire, weavers cutting up their broad looms to make narrow ones.

THE BEGINNING OF SHOP WEAVING IN FACTORIES

ALTHOUGH DOMESTIC LOOMS continued to be by far the most numerous, some instances of looms begin to occur in factories from the start of the nineteenth century.

The German writer Philipp Andreas Nemnich, whose account of British manufacturing was published in 1807, said that all processes of manufacture were carried out at Staverton factory *except weaving*. It therefore comes as a surprise that, in spite of his doubts about the economics of building a weaving shop expressed in 1803, by the time of his bankruptcy at Staverton in 1812, John Jones had erected a building next to his factory 144 feet long by 30 feet wide of three floors, the upper two of which were used as weaving shops. After the factory had been sold, the new owner Joyce, Cooper and Co. held a sale of surplus materials including iron gear for 40 spring looms.

From this time onwards, it is clear that some clothiers set up facilities for a limited amount of weaving to be done on their own premises, often associated with the use of spring looms. Also in 1812, there were eight Daniel patent looms in a factory at Stoney Littleton. By 1818, there were 30 spring looms at Bridge Mill, Trowbridge. Batheaston factory had 14 broad spring looms in 1823. This trend continued. By 1829 there were 10 spring looms at Freshford factory and in 1841, 19 broad looms at Greenland Mills in Bradford.

The probable benefits to clothiers in moving to shop weaving were that they could pay journeyman's rates to weavers (3d or 4d less than cottage weavers per yard) and that they could ensure that weavers could be kept at work instead of drifting off to the ale house or the local fair, a constant complaint of clothiers. They also had capacity in house in case there was a flush of trade to prevent, as far as possible, the necessity of going round the villages to find people able to take chains.

There were good examples of weaving shops belonging to factory owners in the High Street at Chapmanslade.

Chapmanslade. We must thank the forgotten genius who dated this building by inserting bottles with their ends showing in the wall to the left, even if he didn't understand Roman numerals – MVIIIXXI, by which they meant 1821. Records at Longleat show that it was used, no doubt as a weaving shop, by J. and J. Cockall of Boyers Mill, Westbury Leigh

Further along the street in Chapmanslade is this building to which John Hooper Taunton was admitted as copyhold tenant in 1822. A survey of 1828 describes it as a weaving shop. Taunton died in 1848, and it was offered for sale in 1850 as a well-built weaving shop of three floors thirty feet by twelve feet, each capable of taking two broad looms. The building still stands but has been much altered.

This hand loom went round in the Frome diamond Jubilee carnival of 1897 to illustrate the methods of 1837. It does not seem to have the cords necessary to make it a spring loom. This is not of, of course, conclusive evidence. The woman sitting beside the loom is using a quilling turn to wind bobbins for the shuttle. For a clear picture of the cordage on a spring loom see the illustration on page 5.

THE REVIVAL OF THE FANCY TRADE

A PART FROM NAISH's business in Twerton which ended in 1817 and Waylen's at Devizes which ended in 1821 production of cloth in this area seems to have been entirely limited to plain colours for some years. This is borne out by sales of cloth and clothier's goods which appeared from time to time and also by Edward Baines's *The Woollen Manufacture of England with Special Reference to the Leeds Clothing District,* published in 1858.

> For the first thirty years of this century, the woollen manufacture was confined almost altogether to plain cloths and cassimeres, generally in self colours, with a few grey mixtures. About 1830 what are called fancy trowserings came into pattern. In a very few years, however, the variety of design and colouring became much greater and more pronounced; but these fancy goods were confined to trowserings, and in Yorkshire the trade was confined to the Huddersfield

district. Soon figured woollens began to be used for morning coats as well as for trowsers, and then they were applied to ladies' mantles. The use of these fancy goods for coats gave a heavy blow to the plain cloth trade, in which the West of England and Leeds manufacturers were principally engaged. The plain cloth trade now forms a much less important proportion of the trade than was the case fifteen years ago, and fancy goods are coming more and more into use.

During the past few years there has been some revival of the plain cloth trade; but it has only been slight, and is principally owing to the exceptionally low price of wool during the last two years. In fancy woollens there has been very great improvement during the last fourteen years, especially in the kinds used for ladies' mantles. Formerly this trade was merely a variety of figures, but designs are now commonly made which would then have been deemed impossible, at all events without a very heavy cost.'

Baines goes on to describe how the Yorkshire manufacturers had developed the fancy trade by the use of cotton and worsted warps, which had enabled them to use a much lower quality of wool. They could produce really handsome goods at a surprisingly low cost, and brought their use within the means of the poorest.

In 1840, the Parliamentary Report on Handloom Weaving by Anthony Austin was published. This shows clearly that by that time manufacturers in Trowbridge and Westbury had moved into the fancy trade on a considerable scale, with small quantities at Frome, Melksham, and Calne. When the fulling mill at Bulkington was advertised in 1848 it was said to be well placed for the fancy goods trade so extensively carried on at Trowbridge.

We have no evidence of use of cotton and worsted warps in the West of England trade. It sounds like an expedient that would have been left to Yorkshire clothiers!

Baines has nothing to say about the technical advances which made

A loom fitted with a witch.

fancy weaving easier. For these, we can turn to another Yorkshire source. In W. B. Crump and Gertrude Ghorbal's *A History of the Huddersfield Woollen Industry,* published in 1935, they tell us that the local newspaper reported in October 1829 that one branch of the fancy trade had been considerably revived by the introduction of a machine called a witch. This was a device fitted to a loom which pre-determined the sequence in which the harnesses were raised and lowered, and so enabled the weaver to produce a complex pattern simply by working two treadles. The witch would control up to about 40 harnesses.

It was soon joined, and ultimately replaced, by a similar device called a dobby, invented by Joseph Senior of Dalton and his foreman Thomas Brooke. This enabled up to 160 harnesses to be used. Jacquard looms, in which the warp is controlled by means of punched cards, were also in use in Yorkshire in the 1830s. By using these methods vestings and waistcoatings displaying flowers and sprigs were introduced into the Huddersfield trade. The pre-selectors - witches, dobbies and Jacquard motions – all made it possible to weave a complex pattern using a loom with only two treadles.

A loom fitted with a dobby. The dobby uses a chain of bars, each bar having pegs on it. As the chain moves it controls the harnesses.

It is curious how the introduction of the witch and the dobby into handloom weaving has escaped the notice of textile historians such as Miss

Mann both in her principal book and in the *History of Technology*, and David Jenkins and Ken Ponting in their *British Wool Textile Industry*. J. G. Jenkins in *The Wool Textile Industry in Great Britain* only mentions the dobby as a component of the power loom; in his *Welsh Woollen Industry*, however, he describes a dobby loom.

In all the sources I have used I've only ever seen the word witch twice. One comes from as late as 1878, when a Stroud firm advertised in the Trowbridge paper for a pattern weaver accustomed to work a witch. This suggests that it was a skill not very often found, but this is too late to affect the present discussion. It seems odd that they did not purchase another loom instead.

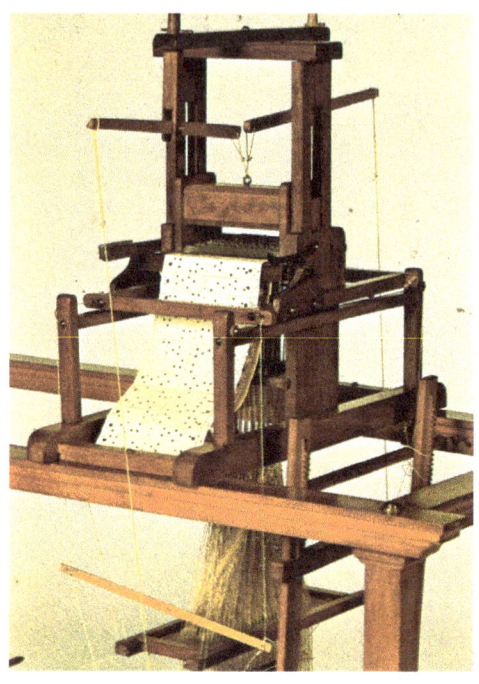

A Jacquard loom, which uses punched cards to control the harnesses. The device could be considered a very early form of computer.

At a sale of the goods of John Stancomb and Sons at Castle Factory, Trowbridge in 1858 were 17 looms with witch and Jacquard fittings and numerous sets of fancy harness. There is no indication that these were power looms.

In view of the conservative attitudes exhibited towards the use of the spring loom, it seems unlikely that the use of a witch or other form of preselector would have been readily accepted. We should also note that the addition of a pre-selector increased the height of a loom beyond that which would fit into many cottages.

In his 1840 report on hand loom weaving Anthony Austin gives us specific information. In discussing the price paid for Cassimeres, he tells us the time taken to weave a piece was longer because the yarn is generally spun smaller, put four into a division of a slay instead of two and so breaks more frequently and the treadles are more numerous to produce the twill and the feet have to be shifted at each tread.

Talking about Gloucestershire, he says fabrics recently introduced called doeskins were woven on looms with eight treadles. In this Gloucestershire section he tells us

'Weavers are jealous of any alteration and unwilling to be put out of their way'

This is borne out by the reminiscences of James Allen of Bradford who in 1930 was interviewed by the *Wiltshire Times* about his childhood in a weaving family. His father would repeat

> 'Look behind, look here and there
> Between the harness, everywhere
> If anything wrong should chance to be
> Then you have your eyes to see'.

He then went on 'the weaver had sometimes to manipulate seven treadles' – so he clearly did not have a pre-selector device of any kind. This may be the seven harness doeskins that were shown at the London Exhibition of 1871.

Trowbridge firms showed a wide variety of cloths in the Great Exhibition of 1851. Salters' fine woollen trouserings included fancy plaids, ribbed checks, fancy elastic and elastic Angola. Clarks made patent beaver, Venetian, and ladies' cloth, John Stancomb and Son fancy moleskins and Angolas, twilled buckskins, and Imperial cloths for summer coats, and W. and J. Stancomb single elastic and single moleskins of fancy texture. Made at Trowbridge and exhibited by a London wholesaler were Clarendon cloths for summer paletots and fancy doeskins of new designs for pantaloons.

Equally puzzling descriptions of cloth appeared in the catalogues for later exhibitions. At the Paris exhibition of 1855, John Stancomb and Sons, W. and J. Stancomb, and Salters all showed fancy trouserings, but the judges noted that there was little novelty of design in the West of England cloths. In 1862 Salters and W. and J. Stancomb were commended for good and tasteful fancy cloths at medium prices. In the exhibition of 1871 several Trowbridge firms were mentioned as producers of fancy goods – Clarks, J. Cogswell, E. and J. Kemp, and J. and E. Hayward. The buckskins, doeskins and cords of J. H. Webb and Co. were of remarkably fine quality.

In the Paris exhibition of 1878 Hewitt and Kemp showed a wide range of cloths and Salters no fewer than 150 varieties of plain and fancy trouserings in wool and silk mixtures (for which they won a gold medal). The exhibits of Carr's of Twerton sound even more exotic, including Elysian, sable and fur beavers, Sardinians, and oriental twills.

re J. & E. HAYWARD, In Liquidation.

THE MART, MANVERS ST.,
TROWBRIDGE.

A CATALOGUE
OF ABOUT

8000 YARDS OF
WOOLLEN CLOTH

COMPRISING :—

BLUE ANGOLA,
TREBLE MILITARY STAFF and TWILLS,
BLACK HALF-MILLED DEERSKIN,
TREBLE FANCY, SINGLE FANCY,
TREBLE STRIPE, SIX-QUARTER BUCKSKIN,
MIXED TWILL, BLUE TWILL, BLACK,
HALF-MILLED FANCY AND OTHERS.

Which will be Sold by Auction,
BY

MESSRS. FOLEY & SON,

On Thursday, October 9th, 1879,
AT TWELVE O'CLOCK TO THE MINUTE.

ON VIEW THE DAY PRECEDING THE SALE.

CATALOGUES may be obtained of the Auctioneers, The Mart, Manvers St., Trowbridge.

Auction and Estate Agency Offices,
The Mart, Manvers St., Trowbridge.

J. DIPLOCK, PRINTER, TROWBRIDGE.

The catalogue of the 1862 exhibition has an interesting note about the Melton finish

In 1857 and for some years previously the prevailing finish of cloths and fancy cassimeres was a highly pressed and glossy surface with the wool strongly laid one way. It remained a fashion for a long time, but was hard, and eventually gave way to a softer and more pliable finish without gloss, called the Melton finish, first used in the West of England and then in the North. It has enjoyed unparalleled popularity for many years, first for coats and then extended to fancy patterns for coatings and trouserings of all kinds.

The date 1857 is clearly a misprint in view of the way the paragraph goes on – it must be 1837, but whenever it was, it shows the West of England trade sometimes influenced the much larger Yorkshire industry.

The Revd. John Wilkinson wrote a history of Broughton Gifford in 1860 and unlike many of his contemporary historians and much to his credit, spoke to inhabitants, including a weaver. He was told

> Within the last few years, [cloth] manufactured has entirely changed. It used to be all "broad". Now none is so. The power looms do all this. Our cloth is "narrow", "fancy stuffs" for summer wear, jacketing, trouserings, and waistcoatings.
>
> That the handloom weaver retains this slender portion of the trade is greatly owing to the circumstance, that the master manufacturer doubts as yet, whether it would be worth his while to lay out his capital in the purchase of looms and machinery specially adapted for this kind of cloth. Were his orders greater, and likely to be permanent, he would imitate his Yorkshire confrere, enlarge his mill, and do all there.

This gives a slightly misleading impression – it is true that what broadcloth was produced was woven on power looms but, as we shall see below, most power looms in Trowbridge factories were weaving fancy goods as well.

Three girl power loom weavers, about 1880, holding their shuttles

FACTORY WEAVING: POWER LOOMS

THE INTRODUCTION OF POWER LOOMS IN THE AREA

It would be difficult to overstate the impact, both to the eyes and the ears, of a shed full of power looms working to full capacity, as I saw at J. and T. Clark in the 1940s and 1950s.

The first power looms in our area were at Twerton, where in 1840 Wilkins and Co. had 67 which had been in use for about ten years. They were operated by 50 men, 16 women, and a boy of 17, and were used for making broad cloth. Austin said that they were 'not on the modern most approved plan'; according to Miss Mann the shuttle was thrown by hand.

A four-storey building for 40 power looms was put up at Staverton in 1839. When the machinery there was sold in 1847 it was said that they would weave any fancy pattern. There were eight at Upton Lovell or Heytesbury in the same year. The first in Trowbridge are said (from a not very clear source) to have been some bought at the Staverton sale in 1847 and fitted at Benjamin Cooper's factory, Castle Court Mill, though they do not appear when the machinery there was sold in 1854. Five power loom weavers, all women, appear in the 1851 census of the town. Miss Mann (p. 220) quotes figures that there were 170 power looms in Wiltshire in 1851, and 27 in Somerset.

The certain chronology of power loom weaving in Trowbridge begins with Brown and Palmer. In October 1855 between 30 and 40 power loom weavers, mostly young unmarried women 'simultaneously quitted the factory'... in consequence of some alteration about to be made in the amount of their weekly earnings'.

In 1863 there were more disputes involving Brown and Palmer's weavers. They were started by a proposal by the firm to reduce the rate given to the plain weavers by a shilling for a cloth of 50 yards, and to give the fancy weavers an extra shilling because they had more shuttles to their looms. This was to be done 'at the next change of patterns'. The plain weavers spread the report that there was to be a general reduction. After one day out the weavers went back at the original rates.

A few weeks later the firm tried again, the hands at both factories, 200 in all, turned out, and the sheds were locked up. On 18 July the newspaper reported that the plain loom weavers said that their work was by far the greatest in demand, and the four-shuttle looms worked much less; the four-shuttle weavers supported them and came out too.

On 25 July the report gives a different, and more plausible, picture. The sheds, the largest in the West of England, employed 200 people, the weavers being mostly women and girls. One-sixth of the looms used two shuttles for plain work, for which there were two patterns; on this ten hands were employed, earning 9-10s a week. The remaining five-sixths of the looms used three or four shuttles for fancy work, at which the weavers earned 8-9s a week. All the looms could do the plain work, but the plain looms could not do the fancy work. The cause of the strike was that the fancy weavers wanted the extra shilling, but would not take it at the expense of the plain ones. The firm said that the plain work had always been a bone of contention, and solved the problem by removing the plain work from the shed. It is not clear what this means; did they put the plain looms elsewhere in the factory, or stop doing it, which would have made the looms redundant? It was not until 1870 that the one-storey weaving shed which stood until 1967 was added to Courts Mill.

A photo of one of the sheds at this firm, by then Palmer and Mackay, taken c1900, shows it uniformly equipped with broad looms of Dobcross type.

The next Trowbridge firm to introduce power loom weaving was John and Thomas Clark, and the process can be traced with accuracy from inventories of machinery in the firm's records. No weaving was done at their Duke Street factory, so until 1857 they relied entirely on domestic weaving. Clarks acquired Studley Mill in 1856, and by 1857 had built a power loom shed on the site. They equipped it as follows.

April - August 1857	Ten 11 quarter (99 inch) looms by Schofield. Three had Jacquard motions and seven treadle motions. The Jacquard looms had either 12 or 20 shafts.
December 1857	Six 48-inch looms, four by W. Smith and Brothers and two by Leach. The Smith ones had Jacquard motions and 8 shafts. The Leach ones are not described.

April 1858	Four 11 quarter looms by Schofield, all with Jacquard motions and 20 shafts.
October 1858	Two 70-inch looms by Haley of Frome.
1859	Sixteen 8 ft 6 in Venetian looms, all with 8 or 10 shafts, all by Haley.
1860	Thirteen of the same looms as in 1859
1861	One more of the same looms as in 1859-60, and two 8 ft 6 in looms with Jacquard motions for 20 shafts, also by Haley.

So when the first shed was filled, (assuming no looms had been discarded), the firm had 46 broad looms (11 quarter or 8 ft 6 in) of which nine were specified as Jacquard; two 70 inch looms; and six narrow looms, of which at least four were Jacquard. This seems to bear out Wilkinson's comment of 1860 that the broad weaving had by then been taken into the factories.

In 1865 the weaving shed was extended, and purchases of looms began again.

December 1865 –February 1866	Eight 8 ft 6 in looms with Jacquard motions for 20 shafts, all by Haley.
October 1867	Four 48 in looms, of which two had Jacquard motions for 16 shafts, all by Haley.
1868	Eight 50 in looms, two by Platt and six by Haley.
September 1871 –February 1872	Seven 50 in looms, all with Jacquard motions for 16 or 20 shafts, two by Haley, five by Millard.
1873	One 9 ft and four 8 ft 6 in looms, all with Jacquard motions for 20 shafts, all by Haley

So by 1873 the new addition to the shed had thirteen broad looms, all with Jacquard motions, and nineteen narrow looms of which nine had Jacquard motions. The Clarks stock books show a decline in the production of doeskins from 1785 in 1870 to 154 in 1875, and none from then on.

Clark's weaving shed was the first in the area of a type so familiar in later years – a single storey northlight weaving shed separate from the main factory.

Studley Mill and weaving sheds in 1873

Studley Mill in 1930

THE SPREAD OF POWER LOOMS IN TROWBRIDGE

ASHTON MILL. In 1860, Brown and Palmer added a new factory at Ashton Mill on adjoining land, and this included the weaving shed of the northlight type still standing there (Trowbridge's only surviving one), which was for 200 looms. The following year, Matravers & Co added a weaving shed of the same type at their factory by the bridge in Melksham.

Ashton Mill sheds (furthest from the camera) and Courts Mill sheds in the foreground

We can tell from various sources, mainly advertisements of sales of machinery, the number and manufacturer of power looms in the area, especially in Trowbridge.

At Bridge Mill, Trowbridge in 1897, there were 64 narrow and twelve broad looms. Webbs of Bridge Mill paid £250 to insure an unspecified, but presumably small, number of power looms in March 1858. In 1862 a woman power loom weaver of theirs gave evidence against a fellow employee, a quill winder, who had stolen wool. In 1867 Webbs bought two groups of small houses to the east of their factory, and built a weaving shed. Its gothic frontage bore the date 1868, and was decorated with a carving of a man weaving. In 1896 Webbs corresponded with a potential new partner from Yorkshire, who would manage their business and introduce new capital. He regarded their machinery as in general adequate, but he was particularly critical of their looms. He said that he would require at least twelve new power looms, 80-84 reed space, 2 beams, 4 boxes each end, 36 shaft dobby, and patent taking-up motion. These would cost £70 each. He also required three pattern handlooms, 4 boxes each, 42 reed space, with dobbies up to 36 shafts. The negotiations came to nothing, and when Webbs' trade ended in 1898 they had three broad looms by Schofield and nine by Haley: all but one of the Haley looms had Jacquard motions. Of their 64 narrow looms, 63 were by Haley and one by Millard, and all but three had Jacquard motions. All these may well have dated from the equipping of the shed in the 1860s.

Entrance to Bridge Mill, Trowbridge weaving sheds 1868

At Castle Court Mill, Trowbridge: 1888, there were 15 narrow looms by Millard and two more by Haley

At Cradle Bridge Mill, Trowbridge there were in 1905, 12 broad and 18 narrow looms mainly by Haley and Millard

At Duke Street, Trowbridge (Salter's weaving Department) in 1865, there were 'nearly 100' power looms by Haley. Salters adopted power loom weaving in 1861, when they opened a new shed on a site in Duke Street. In his speech at the opening the foreman said that 'not long ago' they had only one power loom, now nearly a hundred. They were supplied by Haleys of Frome. The report of an accident to a quill winder in 1864 says that about 100 hands, mostly female, were employed there.

Duke Street Mill Trowbridge

At Home Mill until 1906 the firm used Duke Street Mill as their weaving department and there were probably few, if any, looms at the Home Mills site.

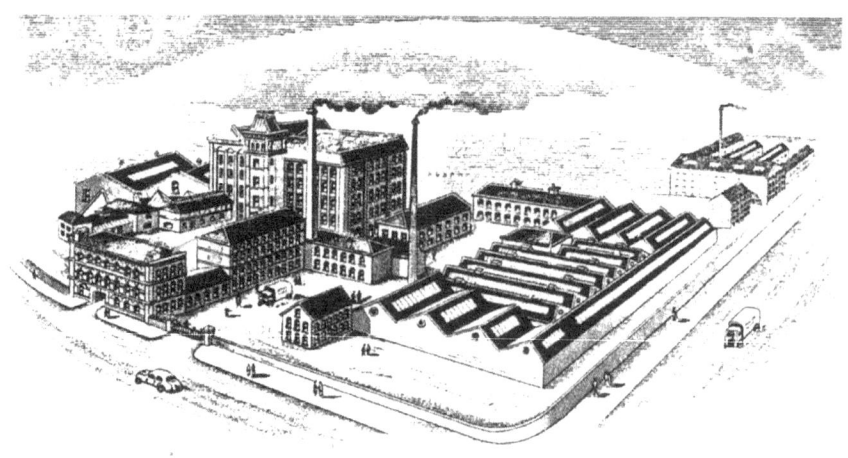

Home Mill, Trowbridge (the extent of the weaving sheds are greatly exaggerated

Home Mill, Trowbridge 1897 giving a more plausible view of the scale of the factory

At Innox Mill, Trowbridge, there were 70 looms in 1867.

Innox Mill, Trowbridge

Upper Mill, Trowbridge had ten broad and 62 narrow looms mainly by Haley in 1867.

After the Salters' fire in 1862, two partners named Hayward left and began a new business at Upper Mill, where they greatly extended the

Upper Mill, Trowbridge

buildings. There is no specific information about when they began power loom weaving, but it seems almost certain that they did so from the start. When they went bankrupt in 1879, they had ten broad looms, of which two had Jacquard motions, and 62 narrow looms. Only seven of the latter had Jacquard motions, but the catalogue shows that most of them had either six- or eight-shuttle boxes. Of the total of 72 looms, 59 were by Haley, eight by Millard, and one by Schofield (remaining ones unspecified). The report of the sale says that the machinery sold well apart from the looms, which were not of the most improved kind.

Yerbury Street Mill, Trowbridge: 1876, 41 narrow and four broad looms mostly by Haley

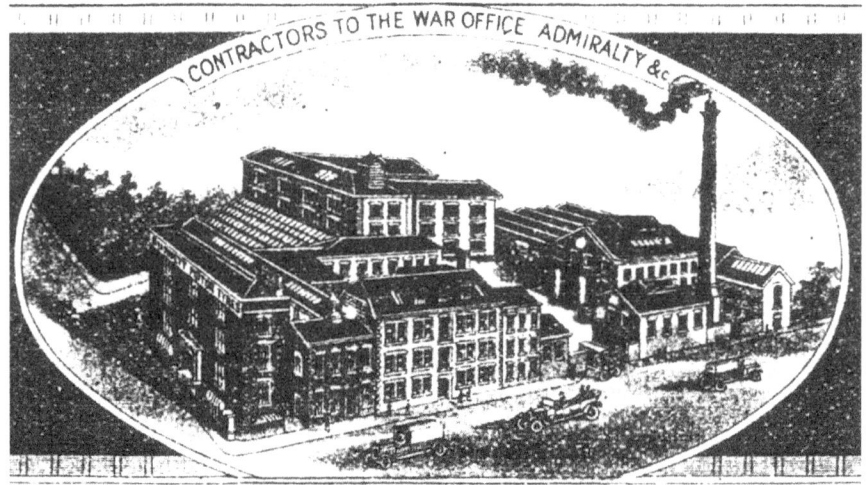

Yerbury Street Mill, Trowbridge

POWER LOOMS IN OTHER TOWNS

POWER LOOMS WERE also introduced elsewhere in the district.

Abbey Mill, Bradford: 1898, twelve broad looms of which two were made by Haley and 49 narrow looms by Haley and Millard.

Boyers Mill, Westbury: 1863, 19 looms. This is known through the account of a dispute between Joseph Harrop, one of the owners of the mill, and 19 power loom weavers who had objected to a boy of eleven acting as timekeeper; he had no clock and often rang the bell before starting time. The weavers were prosecuted and Harrop left the court 'amid a volley of groans, hooting, hissing, yelling and discordant noises'.

Freshford Mill: 1879, twelve narrow looms by Millard.

Holt factory: 1874, six patent narrow looms Millard and four broad doeskin looms by Haley capable of weaving fancy coatings and trouserings.

Matravers & Co, Melksham: 1888, 45 looms, shed built by 1861.

Staverton Factory: 1870, There were 31 broad power looms in the Staverton sale in 1870, by Leach and Sons and other makers. Three had Jacquard motions.

Other firms with extensive weaving sheds of the type under discussion include Greenland Upper Mill, Bradford; Walbridge Mill, Frome and Vallis Way Mill, Frome, but we do not know how many power looms were installed at these. Still further factories must have had many power looms but we do not know the arrangement within the site – these include Laverton's Angel and Bitton Mills, Westbury (an extension to Angel Mill, which was probably intended to house power looms, is dated 1868), and Waterford Mill, Chippenham.

Although details of loom makers are not always available, the records about power looms in the factories make it clear that local manufacturers, other than J. and T. Clark, relied heavily on two local producers of looms, Haleys of The Selwood Iron Works at Frome and Millards of the Ashton Iron Works at Trowbridge.

Greenland Mill, Bradford

A Bradford interior, either Abbey Mill or Greenland Mill

Mill near bridge in Melksham (later Avon Rubber)

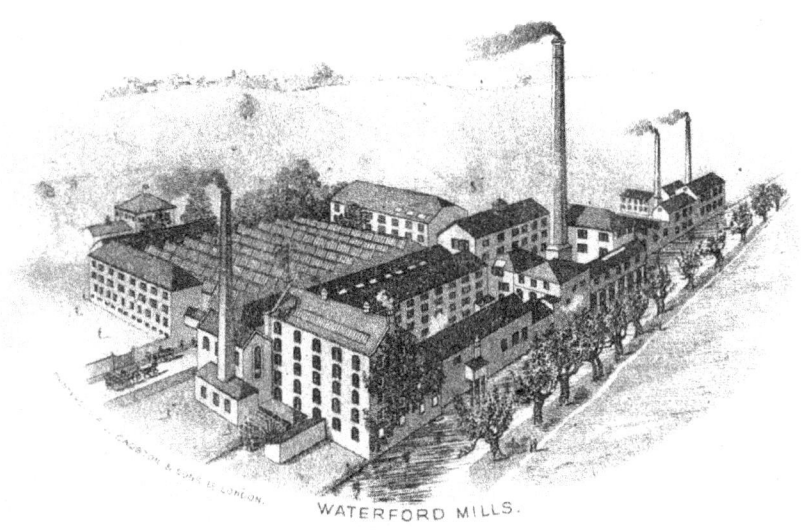

Waterford Mills Chippenham

Walbridge Mills, Frome (the extent of the sheds make it clear that more processes than weaving were carried out in them.

Vallis Way Mill, Frome

THE LAST DAYS OF HANDWEAVING

THUS, BY THE last quarter of the nineteenth century, there were a great number of power looms in the area. The numbers that we can be certain of from the advertisements cited above add up to over 788 alone, and we can be sure that there were several hundred more in factories for which we have no accounts.

So how did cottage handweaving continue in the face of this weight of competition?

Some factories only relied on cottage handweaving during this period – James Wicks of Victoria Mill, Trowbridge, in business until at least 1867 is known to have had no power looms. Moore and Edmonds of Freshford Mill, who had twelve power looms, also carried on an extensive trade for some years until 1879 by employing a considerable number of handloom weavers, many of whom lived in Trowbridge and North Bradley. There were certainly other firms that could be included in this category. The mill at Farleigh Hungerford may never have had any power looms. The picture below shows that they had some hand loom weavers until closure in 1910.

The workers of Farleigh mill

THIS picture, taken around 1900, comes from Mr Bill Tanners, of 16 Marlborough ourt, Chippenham. It shows 1e workforce of the long-since-losed Farleigh Hungerford loth mill. Mr Manners remembers the mill from childhood isits to Farleigh, when he used to stay with his grandparents, who worked there.

Mr Manners said: "My final memories of the mill are rather vague, but I have distinct memories of the mill when I was at the tender age of six, in 1909.

"Mr White was my grandfather and as far as I know was the last hand-loom weaver in the area. He moved into Trowbridge, and he used to go to Semington on a tricycle to teach the inmates of the workhouse there to hand-weave."

The man marked number one on the photograph is Mr Manners, number two is Mr White (both grandfathers of Mr Manners, of Chippenham), number three is furnaceman Mr H. White and number four is Mr Salter, the mill owner.

The mill was on the island between the river and the mill stream. "To the best of my knowledge it was driven by two water wheels plus one steam engine", said Mr Manners.

There were still some clothiers who ran their trades without occupying a factory at all. They could get yarn spun domestically or buy it from firms of carders and spinners, such as those at Bratton, put it out to be woven by hand weavers, and get the cloths milled and finished on commission. There were still several of these small clothiers in the 1860s; Morris went on into the 1870s, as did Edwin Cogswell of Newtown, who claimed to have a good reputation for his doeskins in 1872, but was bankrupt in 1877. He was also involved in a lawsuit over a fulling machine in 1872 in which his counsel stated that he was 'a manufacturer of celebrated doeskins, celebrated not only in the West, but throughout England. His opponents did not agree stating that 'no machine ever made by man is fit for fulling such work as Cogswells'. There is little doubt that his doeskins, whether good or bad, were woven by cottage weavers.

A good picture of the equipment of a clothier of this type comes from the goods on sale following the death of Joseph Stratton in 1838. Making a guess, a man like this might have given out one or two chains each week.

It is amusing to note that in 1803 John Jones of Staverton believed that such small manufacturers could never survive. He asked Francis England of Bradford to take a respectable place in his factory as an overseer. When England replied that he would prefer to make a little cloth for himself and his family, Jones burst out 'Good God, Francis, it is no use your pretending to make cloth except by those who have such places as me'. How surprised Jones would have been to see such small clothiers surviving into the 1870s.

With the introduction of power looms from 1850 onwards, it might have been supposed that handloom cottage weavers might have been entirely displaced, but several factors made the impact of the power loom less immediate. The years 1850-1875 were generally very prosperous in the trade, and even the firms who were foremost in getting power looms were probably glad to get some work done outside as need arose. Brown and Palmer were still putting out work in the 1870s; evidence in a breach of promise case shows that Thomas Pike got outdoor weaving for Jane Gardener of North Bradley in 1874-77, but that in 1878 trade was so bad that outdoor weaving had been relinquished as far as possible. Such was the state of the trade, even clothiers without their own premises were able to continue.

Although it dates from an earlier period, the report of Anthony Austin into handloom weaving in the area was still probably pertinent after 1850. Writing in a time of trade depression, Austin states that 'In the present state of the trade all the work could be done by the masters' own looms, but the system of not supplying the master weavers unless the others [the factory shop weavers] have more than they can do is not regularly acted upon or they probably would not obtain work at all. It is likely that the clothiers felt it would be wise to maintain a pool of cottage weavers to use if trade improved, and possibly an element of loyalty from the clothiers to their sub-contractors. This may well have persisted in the post 1850 period.

> TROWBRIDGE, WILTS.
> To WOOLLEN-DRAPERS, CLOTHIERS, and Others,
> FOR SALE BY AUCTION,
> By Mr. Meritage,
> On the Premises, in the Market-Place,
> On TUESDAY, the 23d day of October, 1838, by order of the Administrator,
>
> THE entire STOCK, and CLOTHING UTENSILS,
>
> Of the late Mr. JOSEPH STRATTEN, Deceased; Consisting of about 50 Ends and Pieces of the best SAXONY BROAD CLOTH, in the most approved colours of wooded Rifle and Russia Greens, Mulberry, Olives, Browns, &c.
> The UTENSILS comprise excellent Beam and Scales, Weights, Whilley and Stand, a well-constructed Whaum for cleaning Wool, latticed Picking Frames, Baskets, Oil Pump, 2 eighty-spindle Jennies, forty-skein Reel, Sizing Trough, sawed Drying Poles, Spooling Turns, Warping Bar (six yards round),' Skerm and Trough, Glue Chests, Perches with Rollers, Passing Boards, substantial CLOTH PRESS, with iron Screw, Sides, and Lever, Planks, Blocks, &c. complete, Oven for heating plates, Press Papers, Brushing-up Boards, Oil Brushes, deal double Writing Desk, lot of iron Teazel Rods, broad Weavers' Sleys, Brushing Machine, Straps, Turners' Lathe, and a large Chest of Capenters' and Turners' Tools.
> To be viewed on the day previous, and Morning of Sale, which will commence at Eleven o'Clock.
> Approved Bills will be taken.
> N.B. The SHOPS to LET.

The only firm with good archives is Moore and Edmonds of Freshford Mill. When they were bankrupt in 1879, they only had twelve power looms at the factory, and their weavers' book 1868-78 shows that they gave out work to over 60 weavers, many of whom lived in Trowbridge, North Bradley, and Dilton Marsh. The nearby factories at Farleigh Hungerford and Scutts Bridge may well have been run similarly. James Wicks of Victoria Mill near Cradle Bridge had no power looms when his machinery was sold in 1875.

In spite of the comparative prosperity of these years, the condition of hand weavers must have deteriorated. An earlier Brown and Palmer case concerned the suicide of William Read of Ashton Street in 1863. When Joseph Janes, the foreman, gave him some work he said, 'This is something to let a poor old man have [he was 66] after playing for five or six weeks'. Janes said he should have something better next time. Evidence was given that the yarn was so bad that he would have taken five months to weave a 50-yard cloth at 7d. a yard. This seems unlikely. But the episode bears out one of the charges made in the 1863 correspondence discussed below, that the outdoor weavers employed directly by the clothiers got the worst work.

The reminiscences of William Keen, born c1854 at Broughton Gifford, were published in the *Wiltshire Times* in 1933: 'Father used to get most of his warps from Cogswells, but I have known him go as far as Farleigh or even to Freshford when times were bad. Occasionally too we went to Mr. Morris whose place was in Union Street.' They used to bring the cloths into Trowbridge on trucks; if they did go to Freshford it must have been a wearing journey. Young Keen spoke feelingly of the state of the roads which, before the introduction of steam rollers, were simply repaired by spreading stones over them and allowing the traffic to bed them in. [footnote – in Trowbridge were always a pair of trucks like scissors or trousers. This would have been a heavy truck on two cart wheels with a flat bed and sides of nine inches or so which could be removed if necessary. Such trucks were in regular use in Trowbridge in the 1930s for deliveries in the town and by tradesmen such as painters and decorators or masons. Such people would now have a small lorry or a van and if any such trucks survive they are probably in museums].

As soon as they adopted power loom weaving, factory owners would have discarded shop weaving by handlooms in their factories. The weavers, not owning looms, could not join the existing pool of cottage weavers, but probably found jobs elsewhere in the growing factories.

In his article on Broughton Gifford in 1860, the vicar there, the Rev John Wilkinson, may well have been right in his assertion that factory owners were reluctant to further increase the number of looms without a guarantee of a permanent market, but relied on handloom weavers to give additional capacity in good years. Power looms were expensive, and factory owners may well have been justifiably cautious in not wanting to invest when the buoyancy of the market could not be guaranteed in the longer term.

Nevertheless, there was a great increase in the number of narrow power looms in factories during the period 1850 – 1875. It seems certain, therefore, that the fancy trade was gradually taken into the factory as well, and that the hand weaving became limited to the doeskins (said in the catalogue of the 1871 exhibition to be handwoven). It may well be possible, as was sometimes asserted, that doeskins were better hand woven.

From 1875 onwards, however, the West of England trade went into severe decline due to serious competition from the manufacturers of the Scottish borders.

In 1876 the *Trowbridge Advertiser* wrote

> Trowbridge and her sister manufacturing towns have kept pace with every improvement … But in the last year or two the demand for this class of high-priced cloth seems to be declining … the less durable, more fanciful and lower priced class of cloth introduced by the Scotch manufacturers is superseding the West of England … where one piece of West of England is sold now 100 pieces of the lower priced fancy Scotch are readily purchased.

The challenge to the local industry was heightened by the fact that sewing machines were now becoming available in many homes and their possessors were looking for cheap and attractive fabrics. There was also an increasing market for ready-made clothes, the producers of which had the same aim.

In 1878 the *Commercial Travellers' Gazette* noted that the tweeds of the Scotch factories had driven many fabrics out of the home market, attributing this to up-to-date machinery and strict personal supervision by the manufacturers.

In 1877 the *Trowbridge Advertiser* carried an advertisement for a good designer able to imitate and have had considerable experience of fancy twilled woollen coatings, diagonals, cheviots, and fancy trouserings, and a few weeks later another firm wanted a designer for woollen and worsted coatings and tweeds. These were the cloths already produced in Scotland and it is clear that the Trowbridge manufacturers wanted to copy them.

A juror at an exhibition in 1879 commented on the excellence of the West of England products, but thought they should pay more regard to changes of fashion and developments of taste.

These developments led to a contraction of the West of England industry and clothiers no longer needed to resort to handloom weaving as they had the capacity to meet the reduced demand in their own factories. The last example of large-scale handloom weaving that is known was that of Moore and Edmonds at Freshford which ceased in 1879. Their bill heading states that their business was 'manufacturers of woaded wool and piece dyed black doeskins'.

It was not only the handloom weavers that suffered – old firms like Webbs of Bridge Mill and Stancombs of Cradle Bridge Mill closed at this time, whilst the industry ceased to exist in Bradford and Melksham.

No firm reference to cottage or shop weaving on handlooms has been found after 1879. As we have noted above, the factory at Farleigh Hungerford may have continued with some handweaving until its closure in 1910, and this must have been the final end for commercial handweaving in the area. Local factories relied mainly on power looms of the Dobcross type until the end of the local industry in 1982, although a few more 'automatics' were found both at J. and T. Clarks and Samuel Salters.

THE ORGANISATION OF WEAVING

As we have seen, there was a long period where cottage, shop and factory weaving coincided. There is no single source which tells us how this work was organised but some light is thrown on the subject by correspondence following convictions of two men in 1863 for receiving stolen yarn. The theft of materials, often called embezzlement, was regarded as a great evil by the clothiers. In order to understand the 1863 case, we should look at the history of theft of materials in the industry.

THEFT OF MATERIALS

Theft of materials was a perennial problem to clothiers and was the subject of legislation in the 18th century. The stolen material could be sold on to small manufacturers at very cheap rates. A good illustration of the trade comes from an advertisement issued from Calne in 1731; the clothiers and others concerned in the trade there were holding weekly meetings 'to persuade others against collecting, buying, conveying, or using ends of yarn, wefts, thrums, or other refuse of cloth (flocks and pinions excepted)'. Rewards were to be offered for the conviction of both collectors and those who acquired the materials and made them up into cloths.

Trowbridge parish advertised in 1741, asking for help in the cost of a prosecution:

> To the master woollen manufacturers of the counties of Glos, Oxford, Somerset, Wilts, and Worcester. I hope the following account of one of those moths of the woollen manufacture called an End Gatherer, who was punished here last Saturday pursuant to the sentence of the last Quarter Sessions, viz. to be whipt at Devizes, Melksham, and Trowbridge, will excite you to exert yourselves in the prosecution of all such destructive vagrants, who are more numerous in your counties than is generally apprehended….tempting your weavers and spinners to steal. This man, George Moon of Melksham, who had followed this pernicious business for about 30 years past, was convicted for the same crime about a year ago, when…..he had in his possession large quantities of fine and coarse shute and superfine medley abb as well as Corsham blue abb

and drugget shute; with no small quantity of superfine warp, worsted, whole beers of chains, thrums, English and Spanish wool, and ends of all sorts, which goods he has constantly sold to divers persons, who…..have manufactured them into druggets, linseys, rugs…

This man was a dealer in material which had typically been kept by weavers out of the yarn handed out to them to weave, though, of course, some could have been actually stolen by third parties. These goods cost the clothiers from 9d to 5s 6d a pound and were sold from 2 ½ d to 4d a pound.

In 1755 Richard Aldridge of Fisherton Anger near Salisbury, a notorious end gatherer (better known by the names of the Duke and Old Apple Pye) was convicted. In 1777 two men from near Chippenham were found guilty of resisting constables with warrants to search for ends of yarn; it was hoped that their punishment as well as the recent imprisonment of some other end gatherers, and the burning of eight cwt. of yarn in Devizes Market Place would deter others from 'the iniquitous and unjust practice of making up goods principally with stolen yarn'.

In 1785 the *Salisbury Journal* reported that the clothiers of Trowbridge had entered into an agreement to prosecute those found guilty [*sic*] of such crimes. The Frome Society for Prosecuting Felons would give the large sum of twenty guineas for information against buyers or receivers of stolen goods. Advertisements of convictions seem to indicate that the criminals were not simply weavers who had been found out embezzling small quantities – these could be dealt with by the clothiers – but men who had in their possession wool, yarn, and pieces of cloth which they could not account for. Thus, three weavers from Bradford and Trowbridge convicted in 1806 all had wool, yarn, and cloth; it is difficult to see how weavers obtained wool or cloth unless it had actually been stolen. The same is true of the two men named on the poster illustrated. How did one (not named as a weaver) get 54 lbs. of wool of one colour, sufficient to make a cloth, and the other, a weaver, 50 lbs. of abb yarn of one colour, unless they were stolen? This is not the product of end gathering.

In 1814 the authorities at Trowbridge advertised about goods found in the possession of five convicted men, as follows:

James Barratt of Hilperton Marsh, weaver: A Brocolett cloth, No. 1026, 22 yards: a piece of cloth, green and other Colours marked (R),12 yards: a piece of cloth blue and other colours, No. 1025, 19 yards: a Brocolett cloth, No. 1027, 21 ¾ yards: 24 lbs. of yarn of various colours.

William Harding of Trowbridge, weaver: a piece of green narrow cloth, 6 ¼ yards: 167 lbs. of yarn of various colours.

Thomas Marsh of Trowbridge, spinner: a Brocolett cassimere, No. 2214, 41 yards: 34 lbs. of wool of various colours.

David Purnell of Trowbridge, weaver: a piece of double milled black cassimere, No. 2213, 37 yards.

Richard Doell of Trowbridge, weaver: a piece of Brocolett cassimere, No. 458, 21 yards: a piece of Brocolett cassimere, No. 459, 25 yards: 90 lbs. of yarn of various colours.

[*Brocolett is unknown to the Oxford English Dictionary.*]

A sixth advertisement was of three pieces of cloth 'found at various places', no convicted man being named.

As the advertisements asked the owners of the materials to come and claim them, it seems unlikely that the numbered pieces had been stolen from clothiers, either by burglary or rack thefts. We think here we are dealing with people who made cloths from embezzled yarn, giving them numbers to add authenticity.

The best descriptions of such makers come from Stroud. Writing in the 1860s of his young days in the early years of the century, P. H. Fisher wrote:

> The embezzlement of clothing materials and the dealing in them was commonly called *slinge-ing*, and the embezzled materials themselves were called *slinge*. [In these words the letter "g" is sounded like "j".] This offence was very prevalent in the writer's youth: for then most of the manufacturing operations were done in the houses of the operatives, to whom wool and yarn were entrusted for carding, spinning, weaving, &c. And there, as also in the mills themselves, great facilities were afforded for secreting, purloining, and withholding parts of those materials – of which constant advantage was taken; and by which the clothiers suffered great losses. The number of embezzlers and dealers in slinge was also great; and they found ready purchasers in the numerous small clothiers then existing, who worked up the slinge with new materials into inferior cloth.

Another writer on Stroud says that people who kept small mills connived at the activities of the slingers by taking their cloth to finish. The slingers often came into the market with a piece or two of cloth and sold it at a reduced rate.

We have never come across the word slinge in our area, but a very clear example of a slinger comes from an advertisement of 1792:

Melksham. Whereas a piece of narrow cloth, length 21 yards, breadth 13 nails, made with embezzled or purloined yarn, part Spanish and part fine English, of four different colours, namely two plain greens and two green mixtures, made by Jacob Robbins of Chittoe....was seized at Melksham....to which place it was brought to be drest, and on searching the house of the said Jacob Robbins the following day, found on the loomb, a piece of striped cloth, yard wide, 12 yards long, the chain made with fine white Spanish warp, the shoot of fine Spanish abb of various colours; the said Jacob Robbins not giving a satisfactory account to the magistrates how he came into possession of the said yarn was by them committed to Devizes Bridewell for one month. The parties who may suppose themselves interested in this business may see the said cloths at the house of Joseph Saunders in Melksham, and if they can prove any part of the yarn to be their property, may have such part of the cloth.

This illustrates the way in which the embezzling weaver needed accomplices to dress, and no doubt also to mill, the pieces he made. The cloths, made of various colours, would have had to be cut up into short lengths to be sold, which might look suspicious.

In 1803 Thomas Richmond, a broad and narrow weaver of Trowbridge, told the commissioners that a wise clothier could always detect embezzlement by weighing out the yarn skein by skein, and then having the cloth weighed again after it had been scoured and dried. A Gloucestershire wool

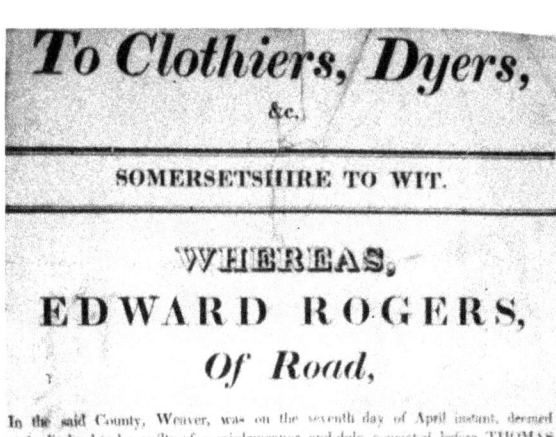

An embezzler banged to rights. Not an ancestor of the authors, but alas, certainly a relative.

loft man said that he always did this. Yet Edward Sheppard, a Uley clothier, said that the principal motive of shop weaving was to prevent embezzlement, 'which takes place to an enormous extent', and John Jones of Staverton said that it cost him ten shillings on every cloth.

A later example of a dishonest maker, in this case called a clothier, comes from 1838. Wool had been missed from a dyehouse at Frome, and John Haines was suspected as a receiver. His premises were searched, and a quantity of wool and yarn of suspicious kinds was found. 'A key of some part of Haines's premises being enquired for....he was allowed to go to some distance from his house to get it, but as might have been expected, he has not yet found it quite convenient to return.'

The possession of illegally acquired cloth, or cloth made with embezzled materials was made difficult to detect because those who possessed it could allege that they had received it in lieu of wages. A good illustration comes from Trowbridge in 1788. William Long of Shrubbs near Freshford was wanted because he had been concerned with two other men, who had been convicted for stealing a sand coloured ribbed cassimere from the mill cart of Thomas Gordon of Stowford Mill. These men 'had been in the habit for the past two years of stealing large quantities of cloth and cassimere and exposing the same for sale in the towns of Trowbridge, Bradford, Frome, and Melksham, pretending that they had received the same instead of wages from their masters; it is hoped that all tradesmen will be cautious how they purchase cloth and cassimere from persons of the like description.' This must have been hard on men who had been paid in this illegal way, to be suspected of theft into the bargain.

The onus of accounting for material found in possession lay on the possessor. Thus in 1841 William Lucas of North Bradley could not account for a piece of cassimere and a quantity of yarn, and was fined £20 or sentenced to a month in prison in default. Of the fine, £10 went to the clothier, J.H. Webb, and £10 to the poor of the parish. A strange case comes from 1842; Joseph Scott of Trowbridge was informed against by Bladud Cuzner, and was found to be in possession of no less than 36 lb. of yarn; it is hard to see how he had acquired so much without being detected, or what he intended to do with it.

By the time of the correspondence of 1863 described below, dealing in goods for recycling was big business in Trowbridge. Those engaged in it were called marine store dealers. Two appear in the 1859 directory, George Hillier of Timbrell Street and Mrs Sarah Clift of Mortimer Street. We can tell that Hillier's business was extensive, from the size of his now-disappeared warehouse at the corner of Timbrell Street and Prospect Place and from the

George Hillier's warehouse at the corner of Timbrell Street and Prospect Place, 1960s

still-standing warehouse that he built in Back Street at about this time.

The trade of the marine stores dealers was a perfectly legitimate trade in waste materials, as is shown by James Harris's advertisement of 1861. Yarn could be used by a clothier; a typical recipient would be one of the small, 'non-factory' clothiers of whom there were still several in Trowbridge at this time, such as Joseph Walker of Ashton Street.

The marine stores dealers were not always on the right side of the law, however. George Hillier was involved in a receiving case in 1861 when he bought, for £2, 76 pounds of best German fleece wool worth £5 10s which had been stolen from Sheppards

JAMES HARRIS,
Woollen Waste and Flock
DEALER,
FURNITURE BROKER, &c.,
MORTIMER STREET, TROWBRIDGE.

A large Stock of Household Furniture always on hand, at the lowest possible prices.

BEDS READY MADE, & FLOCKS & MILLPUFFS
WHOLESALE & RETAIL.

James Harris's advertisement of 1861

of Frome. In another case in the same year Clarks prosecuted a boy seen taking a basket suspected to contain yarn from their Duke Street factory to Mrs Clift and to George Sidnell, a marine store dealer (though described as a broker in the directory) in Back Street. The boy said the basket only contained rags, and no yarn was found at the dealers' premises, so he was discharged.

In both these cases the accused were the suspected thieves rather than the receivers. In 1858, however, Simon Harper of Trowbridge was fined at Wotton-under-Edge for buying 40 pounds of yarn from two weavers in the employ of Long and Co. of Charfield Mill, Gloucestershire; he paid 30s for what was worth, said Longs, at least £10.

THE PROSECUTION OF 1862

IN 1862 THERE were two significant prosecutions of dealers in waste in Trowbridge for receiving embezzled material. This gave rise to lengthy correspondence the next year in the *Trowbridge Advertiser*, and although it is too protracted and repetitive, and contains too much in the way of personalities, to reproduce verbatim, it sheds light on the way that the trade in shop and cottage weaving was organised.

Two men were charged with receiving a quantity of woollen yarn, William Bray and James Rodway. Bray, an elderly man, was charged with being found in possession of 28lb. of woollen yarn and cassimere, whilst Rodway, a collector of rags and waste, was charged with having 42lb of woollen yarn in his house in Prospect Place. Several bags were produced by the police; the material appeared to have been cut up to make waste.

Inspector Thatcher of the Trowbridge police said that he had seen Bray's son Albert with the goods on a pair of trucks, and was taking it to Mr Walker's in Ashton Street. Walker was one of the clothiers in the town who did not have a factory. Thatcher subsequently ascertained that it was the property of Messrs Webb and Sons. William Bray said that he had bought it. The waste of various colours had apparently been cut up.

Thatcher went to Rodway's house to search for yarn suspected to be stolen. Mrs Rodway said there was none in the house. They searched and found the yarn in different bundles in a tub in a bedroom.

Both H. P. Webb of Webb and Sons and W. R. Brown of Brown and Palmer identified the yarn as originating from their respective factories due to the consistency, colour and weave. Both stated that the waste should have been returned to them by the outdoor weavers.

Bray said that he didn't know who he bought the yarn from. As he would not say, he was liable to a fine of £20 and four months in prison. As it was his first offence he was sentenced to a fine of £10 or two months hard labour.

Rodway said that he bought the waste just as it was. 'I cannot tell where I bought it. I bought that thrum in a cottage at Cuckoo's Corner. I don't know who 'twas. I think I know. I beant sure. I never thought there was any harm in buying a bit of waste. I've never been before a magistrate before. Mr Moore's weavers at Farleigh and Mr Wicks's never bring back their thrums'.

J. Janes, foreman at Brown and Palmer's for eighteen years said that it was the rule for weavers to bring back their thrums. This was done by outdoor weavers, not indoor. Rodway received the same sentence as Bray.

The material which Bray was taking to him included doublers, yarn which could be used immediately. Rodway's also included some yarn, cut up according to Brown; this suggests that it was stolen and cut up to make it look like weaver's waste. Thrums, however, were only re-usable if they were torn up. Brown said that his firm either did this or sold them. By this time there were several local firms re-processing rags to make flock for bedding and furniture, and also 'shoddy' for re-spinning into yarn. William Wilkins and H. M. Dunn, both of Trowbridge, occupied factories at Bradford in the shoddy trade in the 1860s.

James Rodway lived in Prospect Place with his wife and nine children in the 1861 census; he was described as a hawker. One of them, Jabez, who was an errand boy at the time went on to become an eminent historian, naturalist and author, specialising in Guyana under the name James Rodway. James Rodway (spelt this time Rodaway) was in trouble again in 1867. Superintendent Harris saw him in the house of Eliza Mitchell, a marine store dealer of Frog Lane. He had brought a bag of waste which he did not account for beyond saying that it did not belong to anyone in Trowbridge and was 'not the same as last time'. Harris could not give any real reason why he suspected that it was embezzled. Jesse Biggs, a foreman at Clarks, said that such yarn was not the perquisite of the weaver, the bookkeeper, or the foreman of any Trowbridge firm. The magistrates thought the case was suspicious but dismissed it.

Mrs Mitchell was then tried. Thrums, whole skeins of yarn, and yarn cut up to 'make' waste were examined by Biggs. Mrs Mitchell did not give a clear account of where she got it, buying a bit here and a bit there. She bought some from a man named Harper in the Conigre. On being asked why he did not go to see Harper, Harris said that he thought that that was Mitchell's business. Mrs Mitchell said that she often bought bags of rags and found waste of this kind, including skeins of yarn, at the bottom.

Mr Stancomb – Do you go about buying these things?

Defendant – No, Sir. I am a marine store dealer.

Mr Stancomb – You are open to a great deal of temptation in that business.

The case was dismissed.

William Bray lived in British Row with his wife and four children and was described as a labourer.

Both Rodway and Bray appear to have behaved honourably in the 1863 case in that they did not reveal the sources from which the materials came.

The first letter in the correspondence below makes the point that it would be difficult for the dealers to distinguish between waste legitimately possessed and waste embezzled. Nobody in the correspondence seems to have made the further point that in factories where there was a definite rule that thrums and waste should be returned, somebody should have checked that this rule had been complied with.

THE RESULTING CORRESPONDENCE

THE CASE GAVE rise to a lengthy correspondence in the pages of the *Trowbridge Advertiser*. Although the correspondence is too verbose to be quoted verbatim, we have abstracted it at some length because it reveals details of the organisation of the trade at that time.

This correspondence shows that the clothiers' book keepers, who organised the outdoor weaving for the factory owners, were themselves able to employ weavers in shops that the book keepers provided, a feature not hitherto noticed by historians of the industry.

The first letter appeared on 3 January 1863 from 'Like not Like', who pointed out the difficulties that collectors of waste like Rodway faced in distinguishing legitimate from stolen goods.

Some manufacturers will not have their thrums and waste brought back to them. Those who collect waste [people like Rodway] have a right to buy of those [cottage weavers] who have the privilege of keeping it. How are they to know which weavers have or have not the privilege of keeping it? The fault lies with the weavers.

In the same edition there was a letter from 'W O I', who introduced another theme of the correspondence, the practice of the factory owners paying their book keepers a low wage but allowing them to make it up by themselves employing journeymen weavers in shops which the book keepers provided.

W O I alleges that this system is perpetuated by the book keepers to prevent manufacturers bringing all work into factories to be done by power looms.

> Nine tenths of the foremen in this town receive no more than £1 or 30s per week direct wages. The masters imagine they cannot afford to pay them more, and so resort to the ruinous practice of giving them so many strokes of weaving [we discuss strokes in more detail later]. They then look out for weavers who will weave it under price, and give 2d, 3d, or 4d a yard less for weaving than the masters would. 3d at 50 yards is 12s 6d. How can any weaver afford to weave 50 yards at 12s 6d less than the master's price and do it honestly? They can find no way of making up this deficiency except by stealing yarn. The foremen overlook deficiencies in the weaving because they are afraid of being deprived of their strokes.
>
> Manufacturers, if you wish for new machines for every sort of work, end this system. As long as you pay the foremen in strokes, your new machines will never be able to do some of your work. Stop it, and in twelve months you will find these machines will be able to do any of your work.

In the next edition of the *Advertiser* on 10 January 1863, 'A Lover of Truth' presents a cogent defence and explanation of the book keepers, of whom he is one himself. In particular, he argues that his journeymen weavers working in his weaving shop are better off than the master weavers in the cottages as they are assured of a regular supply of work.

Lover of Truth goes on:

> The qualifications for a foreman of weavers, or weavers' book keeper are:
> 1. He must know how to make the yarn into all kinds of fancy patterns
> 2. He must be able to give directions to the slubbers [who made a slackly twisted yarn ready for spinning] and spinners how the yarn is to be made, as to size, hardness, and twist, each pattern requiring a different kind.
> 3. He must be able to divide each colour of wool into the different quantities and sizes for the various patterns.
>
> The slubbers and spinners could not do this, but the weavers' book keepers are bound to. In addition, they must be steady, trustworthy men, capable of reading and writing.

He went on to argue that a man who could give such directions would be drawn from the most intelligent of the weavers and it was only reasonable for him to be allowed to employ their families and sometimes journeymen.

'The manufacturers have very wisely allowed them to retain their turns, and have allowed them to have more, to stimulate them to greater exertion for the good of the trade, seeing how much depends on their zeal and activity.'

Lover of Truth was highly critical of W O I:

> W O I is misinformed about the rates. I have been a foreman of weaving for twenty years, and I most positively affirm that my profits have been under 1d per yard.
>
> W O I styles our journeymen poor down-trodden weavers, who are the most likely persons to steal and sell the yarn entrusted to their care. Now everything is just the reverse of what he states; journeymen will and do leave any other place, and even give up work on their own account to weave for us; they are better off in every sense of the word.
>
> We, from personal experience, know well their requirements; we avoid as many changes of pattern as possible, and allot to each man what he is capable of doing. We can do this more than is possible for master-weavers to do. Beside all this, we can afford to pay more than other master-weavers, for they have to lose day after day in going about seeking for work, and are able to do but very little with their own hands, while we are on the spot, and are losing no time in seeking work.
>
> W O I says, that, as we have the keeping of the books, we are enabled to overlook many deficiencies in our own cloths which we should not do in the cloths of other weavers. He is entirely wrong there, for all the pieces are passed in a finished state by the masters themselves, and never by us; if there is any deficiency it is sure to be detected by them, and we are shewn and charged with it. He insinuates that the masters are such fools that they do not know what kind of work their power-looms are capable of doing, and that we misdirect them in order to get certain sorts for our own hand-looms; but I can assure him that is not the case, for the power-looms have been in use so long that the masters know their capabilities quite as well as we do ourselves.

Lover of Truth's letter was refuted in the edition of 24th January by A Friend of the Oppressed, who queried the assertion that the book keepers needed to have any part in the production of the yarn and that this was the role of the pattern designers.

A Friend of the Oppressed stated, no doubt truly that 'book keepers' weavers have the best of the work, the power looms the second best, and the masters' weavers [cottage weavers] the worst.' The clothiers should have checked whether their weavers were returning their waste cloth and their not doing so led to the unfair prosecutions of Rodway and Bray. He felt that the two dealers in waste had been wrongfully convicted, a sentiment that was widespread in the town.

In the following two editions, A Lover of Truth identifies himself as Daniel Lucas, a book keeper at J. and T. Clark. He considered that the 'vile scoundrels' should have been more severely dealt with.

In answer to A Friend of the Oppressed's assertion that book keepers did not have any input into the production of yarn, Lucas wrote 'I have been a fancy pattern designer for fifteen years. All that we desire of the designer is simply the pattern together with its tye [the way the warp was set up in the loom] and the warping and shooting [the action of the shuttle]. Then we have to keep the slubbers', doublers', and weavers' books. We have to give instructions about making the yarn.'

On 31 January 1863 Stephen Randall of 8 St. George's Terrace wrote to the paper saying that he was one of the men that W O I had attacked and giving a long list of prices paid by Messrs Clark for weaving narrow goods, demonstrating that there was actually little profit for him.

He concludes

> I have reckoned nothing for quilling and weaving machines, twine, coals, rent, poor rate, taxes, insurance, and responsibility of damages. Now, here is a great difference; 'For the correctness of my statement I refer you to the Messrs Clark of Trowbridge, and to the following journeymen of mine:- Benjamin Lanfear, James Lanfear, Edward Bailey, George Grist, William Mattock, Isaac Parsons, Henry Slade, Samuel Foyle, William Toop, all of Dilton's Marsh [these people were shop weavers in Dilton Marsh employed directly by Randall and working in a shop provided by Randall]. I believe these men are better off than they would be if they had the same kind of work direct from the masters [clothiers], for in that case they would be obliged to come with their pieces which would be a day lost, besides expenses; then if they took back a chain with them (which would not always be the case) there would be another day lost in getting ready for the loom, all of which is now saved. They have no occasion to come with or after their work, which is taken to them and brought back at my expense.

Many of the weavers who worked for Randall had worked for him for a long time and were considered respectable and well to do. He says

> most of these men have given up work on their own account to work for me, and I know they would have but little difficulty of getting work if they left me.

I ask you then to draw your own conclusions as to whether these men have justice done them or not.'

These are some of the men whom W O I has stigmatised as thieves, men likely to steal the yarn entrusted to their care, more than one of whom holds the highest office it is possible for men to hold in a Christian church under the pastor, and whom I believe to be *far, far* above the mean and cowardly aspersions cast on them by an individual who skulks behind W O I'.

I give the lie direct to A Friend of the Oppressed, who says that we do not give directions etc. All wools for fancy and doeskins made by Clarks, from the time it goes in the engines until it is in a woven state are entirely under my directions. I give all orders to slubbers, spinners, doublers, warpers, and weavers.

An illiterate letter from A Z A repeated the point made before that the book keepers' journeymen were ill-treated by being paid at a much lower rate than the book keepers received from the clothiers, but that they had no option to leave the book keepers because they would be allocated inferior work if they did.

On the 14th February, Daniel Lucas wrote

I and Mr S. Randall have always received the same price from Messrs Clark and have in all cases paid the same to our journeymen. We have always paid in cash, the current coin of the realm, the same as we get from Messrs Clark.

I have no knowledge of any one getting anything like the profits W O I has named. Let him give details.

He says, is it honourable to get it done as we do. I say it is just as honourable for a man who understands weaving, to enter into a contract with a clothier, to get a certain number of cloths woven for him at a certain price; the contractor taking all responsibility, and employing journeymen, thereby getting a profit for his superintendence. This is just as it is for a master dyer or a millman to employ people for doing work under their supervision. How is this different to, for instance, a master tailor? He employs men, women, and children, some on his own premises, some at home – but he sets the price and guarantees the good fit etc.

On the 14th February Henry Slade, one of the Dilton Marsh weavers referred to by Randall, wrote to the paper himself.

W O I attacks three different classes – masters, foremen, and weavers. 'I am a journeyman weaver for Mr S. Randall, foreman for Messrs. Clark, Trowbridge, and have been the same for many years. I have likewise been a master weaver, previous to my working for him, and I well know the expenses as well as the profits attached thereto, rather better I imagine than W O I; and I wish to testify that I am better off now than then. My master is a man of integrity and uprightness towards me in every respect. ... W O I has also made a charge against us for robbing our masters, but I can assure him such is not the case.

On the 21st February, a long letter from W O I included the statement 'They have not contradicted my assertion that they are paid by strokes of weaving. The strokes are not allowed to them in order to stimulate them to greater exertions.' We will come to the meaning of this phrase strokes of weaving later.

On 28th February, WOI once again wrote, citing the example of Mr Strong, a book keeper of Brown and Palmer, who had relinquished his right to employ shop weavers in the way described above because he considered it unfair.

If it be honourable, what made Mr Strong, of the firm of Brown and Palmer, give it up, request his master to pay him in wages, and tell him his conscience would not allow him to be paid, as the others are, by these turns? If it be as honourable as a dyer's or tailor's business, why did he refuse it? This noble act of his entirely shivers to pieces your weak and silly arguments'.

'Some of the masters' weavers don't get a chain in three months, and men too who have woven for them for 30 and 40 years, while your men are kept constantly employed. I have no faith in the sincerity of the praise so lavishly bestowed by the letters from Dilton's Marsh.'

'I cannot think how any man can eat the bread which others work hard for. I cannot think how they can dress themselves in broad cloth and their families in the silks which really belong to others, who have worked for it with sweating brows; and when I meet them Sabbath morn after Sabbath Morn, dressed in gorgeous array, returning from a place of worship to partake of a sumptuous repast, my thoughts wing their flight to the abodes of these poor and down-trodden men, whom I find dressed in threadbare and patched garments partaking of their humble meal, then my soul burns with indignation.

Also on 28th February, Daniel Lucas repeated what he said about his agreement with Clarks being for hard cash. He went on to say

If I could have bettered my circumstances by getting employment elsewhere, I was at perfect liberty to do so. Turns of weaving in lieu of wages never entered into our thoughts. There are several men in our trade who are getting turns of weaving, but I believe they are getting as much direct wages for their services independent of turns of weaving as they would get in similar situations in any other trade in this district. After working in my present situation for some considerable time, having convinced my employers that I had a knowledge of the weaving trade, I asked them for weaving, which they very kindly granted. I and my forefathers having carried on for 60 years the trade of weavers' harness maker, making harnesses for all kinds of plain and fancy weaving, I asked the Messrs. Clark for their harness work, and that they allowed me. So you see I am carrying on more than one or two trades, but am I to be blamed for that? or am I alone in so doing? Look around our town to the various tradesmen and see how many of them are carrying on more than one trade or business, and then answer me that question. Let W O I have a family of eleven children to look out for as I have, I think that would make him look sharp enough not to leave many stones unturned, providing he could turn them in a legal and honourable way.

In the same edition Live and Let Live weighed in again:

The case of the weavers is not an isolated one. Are there not others who are deprived of their means of living by the system of allowing foremen compensations or perquisites instead of paying them full wages? This unjust and impolitic system is condemned by all honest commercial men. In other places manufacturers make princely fortunes by minding their own business and paying their foremen to do the same. 'Let the manufacturers destroy this hydra-headed monster, which is now causing so much misery and bringing a world-wide stigma on the name of Trowbridge.

Isaac Parsons, one of Randall's shop weavers from Dilton Marsh also had a letter published the same day. He states that having been previously a master cottage weaver he was now better off as a journeyman for Randall both in terms of income and also because he was now spared the task of collecting and returning his work to Trowbridge. He mentioned that the profit for the journeymen weavers was the same as in his forefathers' days but that for the master weavers had fallen due to increased expenses.

At this point the editor of the *Trowbridge Advertiser* closed the correspondence, which as we have seen had become personal and acrimonious, although in late February W O I had conceded that both Randall and Lewis were by no means the worst examples of book keepers.

The correspondence, if we have interpreted it correctly, shows the organisation of the industry at that time. Weaving was commissioned in three ways. Firstly, power loom weaving took place in factories owned by the clothiers and performed by weavers employed by the clothiers. We are not certain whether at this period the weavers were paid by the piece or by the hour, and the correspondence does not make this clear.

Secondly, the book keepers took on hand weaving from the clothiers themselves and allocated this to journeymen that they employed. This work would have, at least in some instances, taken place in weaving shops provided by the book keepers at the book keepers' expense (this certainly appears to be the case of the Dilton Marsh weavers who appear in the correspondence). The journeymen weavers would be paid by the piece at journeyman's rates. For this weaving, the book keepers would be paid a master weaver's rate but would pay his journeymen a lower rate, allowing the book keeper to make a profit.

Thirdly, the book keepers were also responsible for allocating hand weaving to master cottage weavers. The book keepers' task was to hand out the yarn and to receive the completed cloth back. The master cottage weavers were responsible for collecting and returning their work to the book keepers and would also have to prepare the chains for the loom. Weaving was carried out at the cottage weavers own premises. Some master cottage weavers would employ their families and journeymen.

The master cottage weavers would be paid at master weavers' rates but after the cost and time for transport and set up was included, the correspondence suggests that this rate was lower than that for a journeyman working directly for a book keeper would receive. The book keepers did not make a profit on this work but instead were paid a wage by the clothiers.

STROKES

THE GREAT INTEREST of the correspondence begins with the letter from W O I on 3rd January. He reveals a system of organising weaving until now completely unknown to us – that of strokes. A stroke appears to mean the right to have a cloth woven on behalf of the clothier, so a book keeper who had a number of strokes could allocate at any one time that number of cloths for weaving to his journeymen or to master cottage weavers. It was not only book keepers who could own strokes – master cottage weavers and even people outside the industry sometimes owned them, and could get the work done as they saw fit.

We have only met the word stroke in one other document, a report on the circumstances of a number of people (distinguished only by numbers) receiving poor relief from the parish of North Bradley, which appears to date from about 1840. It is worth quoting from the North Bradley document at length:

> No 15 His son Joseph resides at Bradley, has a good supply of work, has 2 strokes at Mr. Salter's worth 14/- per week, one at Mr. W. Stancomb's worth 7/- per week
>
> No 41 She possesses a stroke of work at Mr Sheppard's in addition to that at Mr Salter's worth at least 5/- weekly. This was unknown to the relieving officer at the time of making the last report. He has in consequence suspended the allowance.
>
> No 28 She transferred her stroke of work to her son William, residing at Whiterow, he is a weaver in good work, lives in own house and lets another…. the stroke of work is worth 5/- per week.
>
> No 60 The pauper has a stroke at Mr. Webb's, only gets one chain in the week, is incapable of weaving himself, nearly blind….. James Holland weaves the work when any.

These entries tell us:

1. That a stroke was an asset that it was possible to set a value on.
2. That it was possible for one person to own more than one stroke, and with more than one clothier.
3. That it was possible to transfer a stroke.
4. That the owner of the stroke did not necessarily do the weaving.

Entry No 60 is puzzling, in limiting the stroke to one chain a week, and in implying that there was not always work. Does this mean that the other strokes mentioned consisted, or could consist, of more than one chain in a week? In any case, a normal chain took longer than a week to weave.

Whether or not this was so, the possessors of the strokes must have made the profit attached to them by having the cloths woven at least partly and, in the case of No 60 wholly, by an employee, in other words a journeyman. The profit would then consist of the difference between the amount paid to the journeyman and the amount received from the clothier. What is not clear from the Bradley document is how the privilege of having a stroke was exercised.

It is possible that something like this system was in place as early as 1803. A North Bradley weaver told the enquiry of that year that 'A great many, several I know, who never wove nor can weave, but carry it on by the help of others, taking the profit'. A Rode weaver knew carpenters and sawyers who kept on weavers and jenny spinners.

The 1863 correspondence only discusses strokes in relation to book keepers. It is probable that master cottage weavers also owned strokes in this period. What is less clear is whether the book keepers used their entire allocation of strokes to employ their own journeymen or whether they used some of their allocation to give work to master cottage weavers. There may also have been book keepers who did not employ journeymen.

A connected practice, which probably involved the possession of a stroke, is revealed by a settlement examination of a North Bradley weaver in 1829. He took a lease of his late father's house at Rode from Mr. Noad, a clothier there, at £12 a year: he did not think it was worth more than £6 a year, but gave £12 to get work. Mr. Noad charged all his workmen who were his tenants in the same way. He said that he did not consider the house to be worth the rent, but the work with the house was. William Miles, in his 1840 report on Gloucestershire, noted that some clothiers would let houses with looms at enormous rents. This would imply that in some cases the occupation of a certain property would confer the right to a stroke.

What we have here is clearly only a partial picture of how the system of strokes worked, but unless further information emerges the system must remain to a considerable extent a mystery.

THE CHARGES AGAINST THE BOOK KEEPERS

IN HIS FIRST letter W O I makes three distinct charges:

1 That the weavers, being paid at a lower rate than those who worked directly for the masters, found it difficult to make ends meet, and so were tempted to steal yarn.
2 That the book keepers overlooked the fact that their weavers did not return all their waste because they were afraid of losing their strokes.
3 That the book keepers deceived the masters about the capabilities of the power looms, because if they were introduced for all the work their role would disappear.

To the first charge, Daniel Lucas, book keeper at Clarks, and Stephen Randall, foreman there, who also had strokes, were able to make an adequate defence. They said that their profits on each cloth were modest. The figures given by Randall include a flat payment by the yard paid to his weavers, and costs of warping, harness and slay, quilling, and carriage which he (Randall) had to meet. It is not clear where the warping was done, nor in what form the chain was delivered to the weaver. In Walker's reminiscences the weaver had the warp delivered to him coiled up, and he had to set it in the loom. Isaac Parsons's letter makes it clear that he did not have to do this. He was saved the expense of playing (the term weavers always used for periods when they were not working) while the work was made ready for the loom – his job was simply to weave it. It is possible that the chain was delivered already warped on to a beam, and even drawn through harnesses and slay, so that it could be put in the loom quickly. This would, of course, mean that each loom had to be provided with more than one beam.

It is not clear how Randall bore the expence of quilling. This was normally done by children, working at the same time as the weaver was weaving, and passing the filled quills to him as he needed them. This was done on a simple 'quilling turn'. Randall may have meant these when he mentioned quilling machines, or he may have meant something more elaborate like those already used in the factories, which filled many quills at once. He may have used these at the factory and delivered the weft ready to be put into the shuttles.

Randall's costs of coals, rent, poor rate, taxes, and insurance can only mean that he provided working space for his weavers, a workshop where several, perhaps all he employed, worked together. Isaac Parsons makes this clear when he talks about his shop mates.

The letters from Slade and Parsons make it clear why they were willing to weave at a lower rate as journeymen. At a time when the amount of handweaving was declining owing to the increasing use of power looms, they were guaranteed as much work as possible (and probably the best work), had it set up for them, and had a place of work provided. The charge that by working at a lower rate they were so poor that they were tempted to steal is not plausible, and in any case could also be levelled at journeyman employed by master weavers who worked directly for the clothiers. The charge of A Friend of the Oppressed and A Z A that the book keeper's weavers got the best work, the power looms the next best, and the weavers employed directly by the clothiers the worst, is, on the other hand, perfectly plausible. A Z A's accusation of truck payment as bribery to get chains is interesting. It would not have been necessary between the book keepers and their own weavers, so it could only apply when book keepers were handing out work to other weavers. It may well have been true with the less scrupulous.

W O I's statement that Mr Strong of Brown and Palmer gave up his strokes and requested to be paid in wages only, and that he did this on conscientious grounds, was perhaps the most telling point made by the opponents of the system, and was not denied in the later letters.

The second charge, that the book keepers overlooked deficiencies, appears to have two meanings. At some points in the correspondence this word means that the book keepers turned a blind eye to their weavers keeping waste and selling it. This is implicitly denied by the respectability of Lucas and Randall and of their weavers, but we suppose may have been true in some cases. Lucas took deficiencies to mean faults in weaving, and said that every piece was checked by the masters, who would be sure to detect any faults; it does seem unlikely that the book keepers would try to get away with below-standard weaving.

The third charge, that the book keepers tried to persuade the clothiers not to go over entirely to power loom weaving by deceiving them about the capabilities of the power looms, could be true. They had every interest in retaining their handweaving. We should remember, however, that they may really have believed that handlooms did the work just as well, or even better, and that this could have been true especially with earlier power looms.

The correspondence also tells us a number of things. It is striking how acrimonious the discussion was and, if the correspondents are to be believed, how much interest the case attracted in the town. The book keepers and some of the weavers who took part were articulate and educated people, and had established positions in society. We learn that book keepers sometimes carried on more than one trade, and kept books not only of weavers but also of scribblers and doublers; Lucas was also conversant with pattern design. From the correspondence we gain an insight into an extraordinarily complex world where modern business practice existed alongside a tradition that had probably evolved over centuries.

THE CORRESPONDENTS

THE W O I of this correspondence was William Walker (1840-1928), later a leading manufacturer in the town. In memoirs written many years later he said 'Some letters I wrote under the initials I O U [*sic*] caused a great stir in the town, ... quite a crowd of people used to be waiting at the newspaper office for the paper to come out on Friday evenings, the manufacturers and foremen sending for an early copy....'. Walker did not remember the points he made at the time about theft of materials; he considered he had been campaigning on behalf of the power loom weavers, who suffered because the bookkeepers kept all the best work for their own weavers. In fact this point hardly appeared at all. He goes on 'After reading the letters, Mr. Brown said to Mr. Palmer he thought I O U was right, and they forthwith ended the system, to the great benefit of the firm and the power loom weavers. Other firms by degrees did the same…'.

Daniel Lewis lived in Dursley Lane. In the correspondence he says that he had eleven children and the 1861 census records ten of them. Whilst three of his children were working then, the rest were still at school. By 1871, he was occupying part (and the major part) of Bridge House in Stallard Street. He was the first chairman of the Trowbridge Cooperative Society.

Stephen Randall was 44 in the 1861 census and had a wife and two children. He was still living in St Georges Terrace in 1881.

Isaac Parsons was 45 in 1861. He was a widower with a 11-year-old daughter. Henry Slade does not appear in the 1861 census for Dilton Marsh.

Daniel Lewis in later life. His reminiscences, published in the Wiltshire Times *in 1911, said that he and his brother were the first people in the town to grow beards at the time.*

OTHER BOOK KEEPERS

THE SYSTEM OF which we have caught a glimpse in 1863 probably evolved much earlier. From the start of the industry in the area the clothiers must have had people who could have been entrusted to manage the cottage weaving. There are references to book keepers from the 18th century.

The earliest example so far found is Henry Usher, book keeper to the wealthy Trowbridge clothier, Edward Horlock Mortimer in the late 18th century. George Walker, book keeper to another wealthy clothier, James Selfe, subscribed the respectable sum of £1 to the defence of the realm in 1798. In 1799 a Trowbridge shearman made Robert Long, James Coles's book keeper,

Daniel Lucas lived in the building which was Bailey's shop by the time this photograph was taken in the 1950s.

a trustee of his will. At about the same time Samuel Tucker, book keeper of Melksham, merited a mention in a directory.

The term does not appear in the 1803 Report, but two men who performed a similar role gave evidence. George Best, clerk to Jones, Hart, Jones and Co. of Staverton Factory, described how he went round Trowbridge, Westbury, North Bradley, Beckington, and Rode to get broad cloths woven. John Niblett of Stroud described himself as a wool loft man. He weighed out the chains and weft before delivering them to the weavers, and weighed the returned piece after it had been scoured and dried to detect any fraud. Like the book keepers of the 1860s he had looms of his own – but Niblett was a man of principle. He could have kept all his five looms at work, but kept some 'at play' [idle] so that he could give work to outdoor weavers whose need was greater than his own.

James Perkins of Trowbridge was the son of a weaver, and he and his wife were described as weavers in baptisms of children between 1813 and 1819. In the next baptism in 1821 he was a book keeper; the marriage certificate of a son in 1838 very unusually describes the bridegroom's father not just as a book keeper but 'Book keeper to Mr. W. Stancomb'. In 1818 James bought a plot of land in Castle Street from Stancomb and built a substantial house on it, and by the time of his death in 1843 he owned about a dozen houses and left considerable monetary legacies. In the 1841 census he is down as clothier, so he may have made some cloths on his own account,

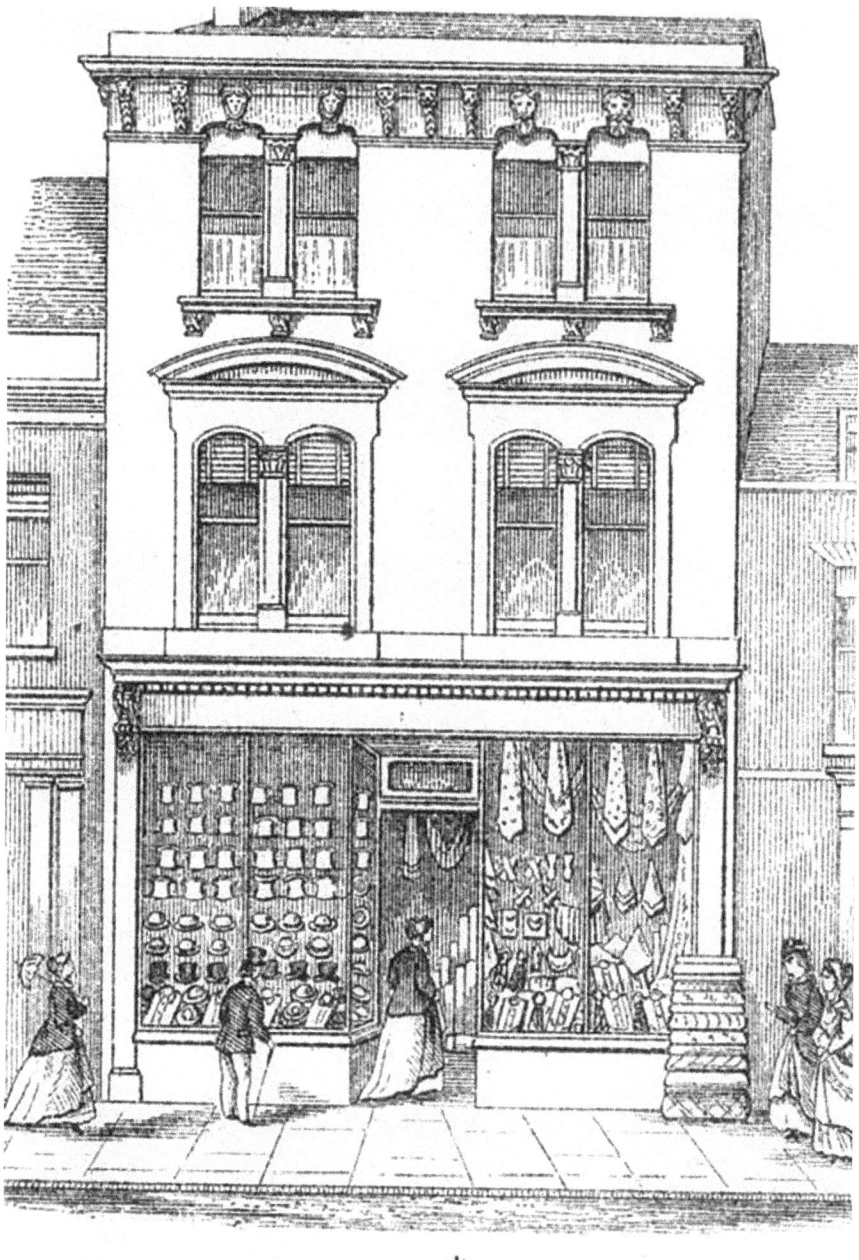

Perkins's house in Castle Street with a later shop front. By the time of this engraving, it was occupied by William Beavan's drapers shop

but in his will he is still book keeper, and it seems likely that he owed his rise in fortune mainly to the system described in the correspondence.

Four men described as book keepers voted in the county election of 1819 – William Wicks and Robert Frawley of Trowbridge, Thomas Chapman of Bradford, and John Mortimer of Chippenham; Wicks subsequently became a factory clothier at Cradle Bridge. John Hayward was described as a book keeper in a will of 1828; when a codicil was added in 1839 he was a clothier and partner in the firm of Samuel Salter and Co.

Only one book keeper, William Deverall of Mortimer Street, is mentioned in the 1841 census. He lived in a large house which had a weaving shop of two floors behind so he may have provided workspace. In the 1851 Trowbridge census there are nine (not including Daniel Lucas, still described as weaver), and in 1861 seven. In that year John Maddox of Alma Street said that he employed four men; he later became a partner in the Yerbury Street Mill. Another book keeper who later had his own factory was Benjamin Perkins, who in 1861 gave evidence about giving out work for W. and J. Stancomb. In 1871 Daniel Lucas, giving evidence at an inquest on a power loom weaver who had drowned himself, said that he had been a book keeper for thirty years.

William Deverall's workshop behind 100 Mortimer Street

In 1865 Clarks held a dinner to mark the opening of a new weaving shed and the reception of William Perkins Clark junior into the firm. In his speech the father of the new director proposed a toast in these words: 'There are others here who are part and parcel of the trade, and without whom we could not carry it on. I allude to the book keepers…'. He went on to comment on the long and faithful service of one of them, John Long Graham, who had died recently, and had been succeeded by his son. In replying, the son, Robert Graham, said that it was the duty of every man in the firm to make the trade as good and as successful as he possibly could, and he believed the book keepers had done this, the same as if the trade was their own.' A later toast makes it clear that the book keepers were distinct from the factory foremen.

Evidence of a close relationship between a weaver and his book keeper comes from the will of a Westbury weaver, John Woodward, proved in 1857. He made Stephen Randall (then still living at Dilton Marsh), 'my book keeper', a trustee of his will.

As William Walker remembered later in life, Brown and Palmer ceased the practice of granting book keepers strokes shortly after 1863 and that gradually other clothiers followed suit. However, until the eventual end of cottage weaving there must have been some system for the allocation of the work, and this must have been carried out by book keepers. There were still six book keepers recorded in Trowbridge in the 1881 census, one of whom was Daniels. Another, Frederick Norris of Ashton Street claimed to be a book keeper at Freshford Mill, although in fact the company had gone bankrupt in 1879.

THE LIFE OF THE WEAVERS

THERE ARE MANY sources which give us clues as to the life of cottage weavers. The lives of shop and factory weavers would have been very different.

The industry was always subject to frequent fluctuations in trade and in periods when it was slack, no weaver however industrious nor any clothier however anxious to keep his weavers employed could go on providing work. The important American market in particular was subject regularly to damaging import tariffs.

After the end of the Napoleonic Wars in 1815, there was a general trade depression which hit the industry hard. By 1816 subscriptions were raised for the poor in Chippenham, North Bradley, Melksham and Warminster.

However, by 1817 things had recovered to such an extent that there was

> We, the Vicar, Curate, and Churchwardens, of the Parish of North Bradley, beg leave most respectfully to state to the Gentlemen and principal Landowners of the said Parish, the present distressed Condition of the Parish committed to our Care. The Parish of North Bradley, consisting principally of manufacturing Poor, is at this time reduced, by reason of the deadness of the Clothing Trade, to the necessity of providing, in a great degree, for the Support of the general Mass of its Population; the Paymasters alone excepted; who feel themselves, for the most part, to be so pressed down by the weight of the Poor Rate now necessarily bearing upon them, as to give them serious Alarm for the Consequences, should not some present Relief be devised for them. The object in view, therefore, is that a Fund should be provided by voluntary Benefactions, for the purpose of employing such of the Poor as are in a Condition to be employed; with the view of taking off from the Poor Rate some part of its present insupportable Burthen; and that the Paymasters may be enabled to bear up with cheerfulness under that portion of it, which they are aware must still remain; till, under Divine Providence, the Times shall change.

> THE PROPOSAL IS,
> That the FUND intended to be raised for the above truly charitable purpose, should be committed to the Management of such Persons, as shall, by the Contributors themselves be judged best qualified and disposed to do justice to them as Benefactors, and to the distressed State of the Parish, for which they are placed in trust.
>
> We flatter ourselves that the above distressing Subject, which has been stated without exaggeration, will be entitled to the Consideration of those Gentlemen and Landowners possessing an Interest in the Parish of North Bradley, to whom it is most respectfully Addressed,
>
> By their faithful and obedient Servants,
>
> Rev. ARCHDEACON DAUBENY, Vicar of North-Bradley;
> Rev. THOMAS TUDBALL, Curate.
> JOHN LONG, } Churchwardens.
> JOB USHER, }
>
> North-Bradley, Dec. 18th. 1816.
>
> Sweet, Printer.

scarcely a weaver not working in Trowbridge or Bradford. By 1820, work was once again short and, to earn any sort of income, people were yoked together like oxen to haul coal from Radstock to Trowbridge, but two years later the factories were working day and night. By the end of the decade wages for both factory workers and cottage weavers fell and William Cobbett was told in 1827 that Bradford factory hands had walked all the way to Heytesbury to gather nuts. The same fluctuations continued in the 1830s and early 1840s but by 1843 the 'Indian summer' of the local industry began and lasted until 1875.

THE IMPROVIDENT WEAVER

There was always a tendency to blame cottage weavers for an improvident life style. Instead of a weekly wage, they would work very hard, for long hours and sometimes keeping the loom going day and night with the help of another family member, for three or four weeks, before they received payment. Then, according to their critics, they would idle time and money away at the alehouse.

William Temple, the Trowbridge clothier and pamphleteer, expressed the view with characteristic venom in his *The Case as it now stands, between the Clothiers, Weavers, and other Manufacturers,* published in 1739. [Manufacturers here means workpeople.]

> The weavers in general are the most feeble, weak, and impotent of all the manufacturers. A male child perhaps is found on a dunghill, nurs'd up by the parish, thro' negligence and want of proper care is weak and sickly, and at the age of 8 or 10 years is put apprentice to a weaver: A parent has a child infirm, deform'd, sickly, weak, and distorted; he considers his constitution, and how easy the employment of a weaver is, and puts him an apprentice to that trade, in which he knows his child can acquire a comfortable subsistence, without the requisites in other occupations of a healthy body and a strong constitution. The father is sensible in this craft his son is not exposed to hard labour, to the inclemencies of the weather, to travel from place to place for employment, &c. He knows if his child is dull, sagacity is not required; if weak, that strength is not demanded; if sickly, hardships are not incident; if slow and unactive, agility is not necessary in the occupation of a weaver: and that by putting him to that trade, he puts him into a capacity of obtaining a comfortable subsistence, with scarce any human abilities.

Temple goes on to make a comparison between the farm worker and the weaver – though he only considers the position of a farm worker who lives in the clothing district, so that his wife and older girls can spin, and younger children be hired out to a weaver (an industrious one, presumably) to quill and wind for him.

> If you will consult the body of one, you will see rosy health bloom in the face, and sinewy force reign in the body, thro' his temperance and exercise, whilst the other is pale, wan, and stew'd by his excesses, sottishness, and debauchery:

one shall have a good warm freeze coat on, while the other appears as ragged as a scarecrow: one shall have his house well furnished with plain bedding, and all the utensils provided by the potter and turner, whilst in the other you shall see nothing but rags, nastiness, and bare walls: one shall have a variety and plenty of provisions, such as bacon, wheat, cheese, and beer, whilst the other has not a crust in his cupboard, nor anything but the pure element in his vessels: the family of one shall be clean, warm, and full of good, wholesome homely food…..whilst the family of the other are poor, empty, and shivering with cold.

Such is the difference between the high paid, idle, debauch'd manufacturer, who perhaps works only two days out of seven, and the low-paid diligent and sober husbandman who labours constantly.

This is, of course, extreme, and hardly borne out by what is known of the lives of farm workers at a later period, or those of some of the weavers of the period. But it is interesting to find Temple's comparison echoed by his more moderate opponent, Thomas Andrews, writing as 'Country Common Sense' in *The Gloucester Journal* in the same year:

In Wilts the poor labourers in villages on Salisbury Plain generally work for 4s. 6d. a week from the end of harvest till the next begins; those in the clothing part as generally have 5s. in winter and 6s. in the summer half year, with the like advantages of mowing and harvest work, and yet 'tis very observable that the poor people about Salisbury live and keep their families in a much handsomer manner than those in the clothing country …. There are not so many alehouses …. every poor family bakes its own bread ….they are freer from the little luxuries which abound among the others ….they are more industrious…..

A hundred years later, Austin, who was by no means unsympathetic to the plight of the weavers, included lengthy evidence from the Relieving Officer of the Westbury Union 1840 Report on Hand Loom Weavers:

[I go round the parish [Westbury then included Bratton and Dilton Marsh, so the comparison is between the two.] One part has only agricultural labourers. Everything is clean and neat, and there is part of a bag of flour in nearly every cottage. In the weavers' cottages the management is very different – they are bad managers. Even when two or three of the same family have work on two or three looms, they are badly off [Here Austin inserted a footnote: they may have been previously without work for many weeks, and be paying off their debts] and the cottage dirty. So eager are the weavers for work that I have known instances of the woman working by day and the husband by night, to get the work done quickly, but when they have work they are not provident......When they bring in their work the weavers are apt to drink, and every day that they look out for work they get together and drink; if they have no money they are trusted [by shopkeepers] if it is known that they are in employment.

The officer then went on to voice a view that Temple had put in this way: 'the poor have such high wages, as furnish them with the means and instruments of luxury and idleness.' The 1840 writer puts it thus:

I have heard and believe truly that when work is plenty the weavers in the Marsh run in debt more than when they earn less, for the females then spend so much in finery that it runs away with a great deal of their money. And the young men dress smart; they seem to think of nothing but drinking and sweethearting. .... I do not know any reason why weavers should be less provident than other workpeople, but it was always so in this parish. They dress very badly on week days, but on Sunday some of the young men dress very gaily, have watches &c. &c. When work is plenty they will not touch a shuttle for a week at the time of the fair. There are three fairs in the year.

But not everyone in Westbury agreed; the curate, for instance, said that the weavers were 'a well-behaved, moral set of men; the population of the parish are generally so.'

In the last days of handweaving we occasionally read of improvident weavers, often when they came to a bad end. In 1861 William Gingell, a Bromham weaver, went to Staverton to see a relative with his son, a soldier home on furlough. Walking back home they were so drunk that they had to support one another; in the end the father was left lying in the road, where he froze to death. In 1862 Joshua Bailey of Dilton Marsh was found lying in the road drunk and totally incapable, with his truck beside him with a cloth on it belonging to James Cogswell of Trowbridge. In the same year Cogswell prosecuted Nathaniel Miles of Westbury Leigh for keeping a piece of work for three months; evidence was given that he was a most notorious drunkard, who had been trifling with manufacturers like this for years. James Francis, a weaver of Hilperton, was a good workman and earned good wages; when he received his money he spent it in drink, then for the next two or three weeks he would stick to his work closely, as an inquest on him was told in 1864. Another inquest was held in 1867 on George Willis of Hilperton Marsh, aged about 50, who 'had lived a wretched life for some time past. His house contained scarcely the slightest vestige of furniture....there was a loom he worked at, and in the corner of the room a bundle of rags which he used for a bed...an old chair.... he had lately given way very much to drink.'

Cases of actual crime could be made an occasion for a sweeping generalization of condemnation. In 1792 an account of the murder of a child and the attempted murder of a wife by starving them at Bradford was followed by:

> It is hoped that this awful warning may duly impress the minds of all parents, particularly those of *manufacturing towns* so that they may feel it not only their duty, but also their interest, to take proper care of their offspring; for which their present fatal addiction to idleness and drinking so entirely unfits them, and by which unhappy propensity their own dwellings are deserted and become loathsome scenes of wretchedness, depravity, and disease.

In 1828, the *Wiltshire Gazette* reported that five thousand barrels of beer were consumed annually in Trowbridge at a cost of £30,000, six times as much as the expenditure on the poor of the parish. The *Gazette* does not give a source for this figure or comparisons with other towns.

THE DEFENCE OF THE WEAVERS

IN SPITE OF Temple's scorn for the weavers, they were anxious to demonstrate that their work had become more arduous and were proud of their skill in carrying out what was an extremely intricate operation. Austin printed *verbatim* a long and rather rambling address, which was in effect a claim for higher wages for doing more work, quoted here in part:

> As facts are stubborn things, let us try to find out a few, out of the many which are existing, which have a tendency to make the poor weaver poorer; and in order to do so, let us go back to the years 1810, 1811, and 1812, and onward for several years. At that time 42 yards, 2,280 threads, 42 inches, 360 skeins of shoot. At the present, 42 yards, 2,480 threads, 46 inches, 570 skeins of shoot, making a difference of 200 threads more, 4 inches wider, and 210 skeins more shoot. Now the 210 skeins of shoot will reach more than 38 miles, consequently the shuttle must travel that immense distance [more].
>
> Another fact is, the warping bar ought not to be more than 12 ft. 4 ins. round, which is now 13 ft. which will make on an average two yards more....

Another fact is, the fancy kerseys [cassimeres] are constantly changing, and scarce two pieces alike for the same loom, in consequence of which there is more time to be lost, more expense, and liable to a host of damages. [*This last point means that the loom had to be set up between each cloth woven*].

Another complaint of the Trowbridge weavers, expressed at great length, was the way in which the trade was 'unprotected', by which they meant that it was not limited to those who had served an apprenticeship:

The work being chiefly put out to people's own houses for ten miles round, hence it follows that whole families, boys and girls, are initiated gradually from their infancy into the trade; adding to this, great quantities of agricultuary families are also initiated into the trade in consequence of the distress among the agriculturing labourers.....

Another cause while many are suffering in the trade is owing to the monopoly among the weavers, and is encouraged by the masters; hence it is, while some are keeping 6, 8, 10, or 12 looms, whilst others, equally as good weavers, are not able to keep on one loom....It is very often the case....that the best hands are out of employ, and themselves and families on the parish, because the men....that have six or eight looms, can get the work done at a cheaper rate by boys and girls at so much per week...

In fact, no source has been found indicating any weaver having anything like twelve looms.

The Trowbridge weavers were at pains to emphasize the skills needed in their trade, and contrasted them with those needed for farm work:

Nor can we think any person in their right mind who would try to put us on a level with out-door labourers, though bye-the-bye we do not envy them, only we wish their wages was more; nevertheless they have many privileges which a weaver has not; first, they are at less rent, they have gardens, which is a great help to their families; they are not confined within doors like weavers, nor do they work so many hours in the day; they have not a thousandth part so much on their minds, but can go to their labour whistling and singing all the day, if they are in a merry mood.

Just contrast this with what a weaver has to mind, with 3,000 threads, and as many eyes for those threads to go through, and from 600 to 800 reeds, more or less, according to the pattern, and hundreds of cords over head and under his feet, and sometimes obliged to count every shoot; these things considered, a weaver ought to be rated amongst the first rate of mechanics in the country.

What the Trowbridge weavers could have added in their defence was that the agricultural labourers had, by and large, guaranteed work albeit for shorter hours in the winter, whilst the weaver was managing a small and highly skilled business, often with irregular work.

Nevertheless, the descriptions of the poorly managed lives of the weavers, one hundred years apart and from commentators with differing perspectives, are too consistent to be ignored. In good times, weavers were amongst the highest paid working people, but there were too often periods of shortage.

The economic challenges facing the handloom weaver may have increased towards the last days of the cottage industry. In his article on the history of Broughton Gifford published in 1860, the Revd. John Wilkinson gives us a vivid description of weaving in the village:

> Our handloom weavers ….work at their own homes in their weaving "shops", many hours for little money. When in full employment they are fourteen hours a day at it, hands, arms, legs, and feet in full play. A good weaver can turn out four, five, or six yards per day, for which he receives 10d., 8d., or 6d. per yard. But this is not all profit. He has to pay perhaps two children, at least one to change shuttles for him. Another child "quillies". Besides, he is subject to deductions for all faults. Nor is he employed every day. If trade be very brisk, he may reckon on five days of such work each week: often he has to be content with three or none. On the whole it may be questioned whether he is better off than his agricultural brother, as regards means of living: in respect of length and health he is certainly in a worse condition. Nor is the prospect before him re-assuring. That he has so long held his own against the steam power-loom of the factory is a marvel to all observers, a strong evidence of his skill, endurance, and energy. Time was, when the weaver kept his pony or hackney on the common, and drove backwards and forwards with his "goods" to his master at Trowbridge in style. Now he is compelled to trudge afoot, driving a pair of hand-trucks before him; and is glad enough to bring back a "chain" after hanging about master's office all day for it.

Wilkinson expresses nothing but approval of the industry of the weavers in his village in keeping a proportion of the weaving work even at this late stage and in competition with the factories with their power looms.

THE PROSPEROUS WEAVER

THERE WERE, OF course, many weavers who did not conform to the stereotypes of 1739 and 1840. Temple himself describes the career of the better sort of weaver:

> Most of the weavers live in cottages erected on waste lands in the villages and hamlets near the clothing towns, or near the habitations of some principal clothiers. When a lad has served out his apprenticeship, in a little time he may either acquire a loom by his industry, or, if he is a person of any reputation, hire or be trusted with one. When he has proceeded thus far, he soon meets with a boy; sometimes from the parish with a sum of money; sometimes from his friends, who comes apprentice to him. This boy in a very little time acquires skill and abilities enough to perform a part of the work in the loom with his master. When he is advanc'd to 12 or 13 years of age, this boy and his master (if the master is as diligent as he ought to be) shall perhaps fill a medley cloth in three weeks, for which the master shall receive of the clothier £1 19s. 3d. or £2 1s. clear.
>
> Whilst the weaver and his apprentice boy are employ'd in the loom, if the weaver has a family, a child of four years of age shall perhaps quill to the loom, and earn 6d. per week; another of six years of age shall acquire perhaps 1s. 6d. per week by spinning; whilst the wife makes her wages 2s. 6d. or 3s. a week by the spinning wheel also; and at the same time performs all necessary offices in the family. Many instances might be given of weavers who in this manner have acquired fortunes from £100 to £500. I would be understood here to speak of the industrious poor, not of the idle and debauch'd....

This is a pretty picture. It relied on a healthy and industrious family of a suitable size, a hardworking apprentice (rather than a journeyman who had to have wages), low or no house or loom rent, and, above all, regular weaving and spinning work.

Weavers of this kind were no doubt among the 120 members of the Loyal Society of Broad-Cloth Weavers who in 1733 met 'according to annual custom' at the White Hart in Trowbridge to celebrate the anniversary of George II's coronation; after dinner they spent £30 in drinking the health of the king and the royal family.

There were many ways in which the weaver's situation departed from the ideal one depicted by Temple. Settlement examinations show many examples of disagreements between masters and apprentices, resulting in indentures being cancelled or apprentices running away. Those who finished their time frequently worked as journeymen; a weaver who employed a journeyman had to pay him a wage out of the money he got for the cloth, and relied on his being industrious and regular in his work too. A weaver's wife might die leaving him with small children and sickness or disability might affect the family.

Yet Temple was correct in saying that it was quite possible to prosper as a weaver. Wills and deeds reveal examples far too numerous to all be mentioned here; we give only a few instances.

James Moor of Lower Studley, broadweaver, died in 1763: he left three leasehold houses there, two of them were let to tenants. A son was left £30 when he attained 21, and a loom, the rent of which was to maintain him until then. £105 was left in trust for another son, and the rents of four looms (three of which were in other weaver's houses).

John Stevens of Studley made his will in 1792. He left five houses at places in Studley, a house at Trowle Common, and two houses in Bradford.

Robert Butcher of North Bradley, broadweaver, made his will in 1744, he left a house there. Joseph Butcher of North Bradley left a house where he lived and a new one he had lately built near it in his will made in 1766. The houses where these men lived are probably to be identified with the pair of handsome brick houses illustrated below still standing in the village, bearing date stones R ^{B} E 1735 and J ^{B} M 1735. (A. F. in his *History of North Bradley* published in 1881 notes that these initials were of Butchers.)

Thomas Coombs of Trowbridge, broadweaver, died in 1759 leaving five houses and six looms. Joseph Sargent, born in 1761, was apprenticed and then spent six years as a journeyman before taking a house at Lacock and setting up as a master weaver c1788-93, then moved to North Bradley where he still continued as a master weaver in 1827.

Prior to 1832 only men with sufficient property were permitted to vote and this excluded the great majority of the population. Voting was carried out in person at Wilton, the county town at the time. In the 1819 county election, 39 voters in Bradford, 25 in Trowbridge, 28 in Dilton Marsh and Westbury Leigh, 10 in North Bradley, and 5 in Hilperton were weavers – and, of course, there must have been others who owned sufficient property to qualify for a vote but chose not to make the journey to Wilton to cast it.

Not all weavers were able to sustain their prosperity. A good example of the difficulties which arose from inability to maintain property comes from a run of Dursley Road deeds. The strangely named Shaphan Waite, broadweaver, obtained a house there by his marriage to Ann Marshman in 1668. In 1714 they conveyed an adjoining house to their son with the use of their pool and house of office, which two others also shared. Subsequent mortgages of the Waite property, increased to three houses, enabled the mortgagee, John Wilson, broadweaver, to enter. He was owed £25 and laid out very considerable sums in

The state of decrepitude which cottages might reach through lack of maintenance is shown here on cottages believed to have been in Wingfield.

repairs and making several useful improvements. On an account with another Shaphan Waite, broadweaver, grandson of the first, it was found that in 1739 the debt was increased to £53. A new mortgage was raised to cover this, but by 1766 the houses had to be sold for £70; of this just over £60 was owing for principal, interest, and repairs, so Esau Waite received less than £10 from his inheritance.

The purchaser in this case was a tiler and plasterer, who retained the houses and let them for some years, no doubt being able to keep them in repair himself. But settlement examinations often show that people who had been lucky enough to inherit a cottage or two had to sell because they could not maintain them. It is noticeable how many insurance policies taken out by clothiers and other tradespeople on town centre properties also include a cottage or two at Studley, probably acquired in a way similar to that described here.

Of course, not all weavers achieved prosperity through legitimate means. This anonymous letter was sent to the Overseer of North Bradley c1840:

> Sir, You Must Excuse my freedom when I State to you A few plain facts which have Come under my notice and several other persons. On the 30 of October Last one of your Popers Mr I Cable junr. Went home Late at night after he had been to your Paye table so drunk that he did Rail from one side of the Road to the other. On the 11 of January he was at the Black Swan inn drinking gin hott and went from there to the three swans inn [both inns in Frome] drinking the same and told the people that he wove is last to chains in 4 weeks and further said that he would weave with any one ther or fight any one there and told the People that Singer [the overseer] Cheates the parish of Bradley £30 in gathering the Rates. The saterday before last frome fair he went to Mr Steeds shop and bought a Large joint of beef and poold out a purse half full of silver to Paye for it the same day as is goods was put down he had one Chain on at home and 3 put out to get wove the trustees belonging to his house forgave him half the Rent he borowed som money of the Book keeper and some of I. Hill to pay the rent and had Plenty of money at the same time the day befor Last Road Revil Mrs Cable find herself sick at the thought of Road Revil her disorder was gon and she went with her husband and abode ther to days drinking and Corouseing at is wifes Last Confinement she had the Charity bag and a Charity nurse given her by the Ladies the worth of 16s and som days 4 diners send her by different People and will again this time at the same time he Came to your Paye table every week for money at the same time he had as much work as he Cold do since he has Paid no Rent he

has bought a new tent bedstead and bed a new top Coat made of the Best Saxton Cloth several new silk hats and a fine watch to put in his pocket he have told several people that he is determin not to Pay any Rent. If you see him on a sunday you would think he was some yong gentlemen instead of a poper on a parish the fact is if he must Pay Rent he now weill that som of his Pride must Com down and that will Go to his……….one of his jurny women work under Price and when she fill her Pice he has 18s Cleer to take you may see him or his wife every Saterday night at Mr Steeds shop byeing a large Pice of meat with is rent money every time that he comes to you he Loses the yearnin of 3s 6d he tell you that his wife is an aflicted woman she is only ill when the Leadies coming Round the district leadies he has as much money Coming in as any weaver to the shop only there is so much Laid out in Pride. Likewise he said that you go about Bradley sundays to the Peoples houses and take of the Pot Lead and see what the People have for diner and that a certain man gave you a good traising ……

APPRENTICES AND JOURNEYMEN

Throughout this book we have made reference to both apprentices and journeymen.

Apprentices were normally children, legally contracted to a master weaver for a period, generally of seven years. Apprentices worked without pay and in return the master weaver would teach them the trade and house, feed and clothe them. To enter into an apprenticeship, a premium would be paid to the master, sometimes by the family of the apprentice but often by the parish from which the apprentice came. This was designed to give the apprentice a good start in life and as an insurance against them becoming a burden on the parish. On completing the apprenticeship, some served as paid journeyman for their master, some left to work for a different master and a few set up as masters themselves.

Not all apprenticeships ended satisfactorily. The master might die or become insolvent, or the apprentice might run away. It is hard for us today to think of boys of 12 or 13 running away, but in those days the great majority of children had begun work by that age.

Journeymen were paid employees of the master weaver. To gain the skills for their job, journeymen would normally either have been apprenticed to a master weaver or learned from their own family.

Apprentices were often apprenticed to masters outside the parish where they had formerly lived. The Poor Law until 1835 meant that poorer people moving to a new parish were examined to establish their 'settlement' – that is to say, which parish should be responsible for poor relief if they were to fall on hard times. The settlement examinations often give a fascinating insight into the lives of the examinee at a time when little information was recorded about most working people. Good and bad relationships between masters and apprentices are illustrated in profusion in the settlement examinations of the parishes of Bradford and Trowbridge.

Robert Simms was born in Steeple Ashton in 1738 and apprenticed to Robert Sartain of Trowbridge, weaver, when he was nine. After five years with Sartain he ran away and worked as a journeyman weaver for other masters for five years. When Sartain tracked him down, Simms ran away again and joined the army until he was discharged nine years later. He then married a Westbury woman who succeeded to a house in Dilton Marsh where they remained until poverty forced them to relinquish it. In due course, Westbury parish removed him to Trowbridge where he was settled in Poor Law terms.

William Strawberry of Bulkington was apprenticed by the parish to a weaver in Melksham in 1747. After three years, his master died, and Melksham parish, now responsible, apprenticed him to Walter Blanchard of Bradford for a further seven years. Unusually in this case it was the master that ran away after a year and a half; to escape his debtors Blanchard went to Wilton leaving poor William alone, until he too went to Wilton and found Blanchard where he continued his apprenticeship for a year and a half. Blanchard then returned to Bradford with an agreement that William should send him half a guinea for each cloth that he worked. William refused and an announcement was made in Wilton that no one should employ him, as he was a runaway apprentice.

Examples of ill treatment of apprentices are occasionally found in newspaper reports. An inquest in 1806 on the death of James Bricker, aged less than 12, found that he had been 'used with much severity by one Vince, a weaver and his wife, but by the testimony of surgeons and other evidence they were discharged of maliciously destroying him'.

In 1743/4 Cornelius Matthews of Bradford was committed to gaol charged with starving his apprentice to death. Charges like these would have been difficult to prove in court but the example in the cutting illustrated below was evidently so atrocious that it was widely reported in newspapers throughout the country.

> Thursday was committed to Salisbury gaol, Joan Edwards, wife of a broad-weaver at Studley, in the parish of Trowbridge, Wilts, charged on the Coroner's inquest with the wilful murder of Margaret Puckeridge, their apprentice from the parish of Somerton in this county, by beating her in so barbarous a manner, that her skull was fractured, and her body bruised all over.—It appears that this inhuman wretch (who has four small children) treated the deceased with the greatest cruelty during the whole time she was with her; she gave her food scarce sufficient to sustain life, and several times compelled her to eat her own excrements. The husband is absconded.—They had another apprentice girl from the above parish, who was treated in the same inhuman manner, and is now so dangerously ill that her recovery is doubtful.
>
> *Bath Chronicle 27 February 1772*

The situation of an apprentice so far away from any family or friends must have been particularly sad even where the master was kind. My own four-times great grandfather, Michael Dorrington, was apprenticed from Mere to North Bradley at the age of 9. It must have been horrible to be taken over twenty miles away into a strange home and unfamiliar surroundings. We know nothing about how he was treated by his master, but he settled and had a family in North Bradley.

Of course, many of the cases that were reported by newspapers or parish authorities were when something went wrong, but it is likely that many others were happy arrangements.

THE FACTORY WEAVER AND THE FACTORY OWNERS

LESS IS KNOWN about the lives of the factory weavers, because it is difficult to separate them from the general workforce in an area where thousands of people worked in factories, and theirs was just one role of many.

Although the Royal Commission of 1833 on the Employment of

Children in Factories visited several Trowbridge firms, their enquiries were not particularly relevant to those handweavers who worked in shop within the factories. Their hours cannot have been governed in the same way as the other factory workers, by the hours in which the factory engine was running. There were, of course, no power looms in the area at the time.

Before the introduction of power looms into the factories, it is likely that the workforce was very largely, if not exclusively, male. This changed as the weavers operating the power looms were largely women, mainly young, from the very beginning. This must have resulted in a significant shift in the economic and social structure of the towns. This pattern of employment continued until the end of cloth production in the area in 1982.

Inevitably, disputes between employer and employee, particularly about wages, arose from time to time, but there were remarkably few strikes in Trowbridge at least, considering the number of factories in the area. We will refer to the strike at Matravers and Overbury in Westbury in 1829 later, but there were strikes at Brown and Palmer in 1853 and 1863 which were quickly ended by the firm making concessions to the strikers.

In October 1859 'A Bradford Weaver' wrote to the paper commending the generosity of Mr Edmonds of Bradford, who had increased the rates of his handloom weavers by 1d, and for some kinds of work, by 2d a yard, and of his power loom weavers by ½ d a yard. This produced a rather tart reply saying that it only brought the Bradford rates up to those paid in Trowbridge.

The clothier Joseph Harrop of Westbury was not a popular figure. In 1863 he took nineteen striking weavers from his Bowyer's Mill to court; they had objected to a boy of eleven acting as timekeeper and since he had not been provided with a clock, often rang the bell before starting time. Although the weavers were fined, Harrop left the court 'amid a volley of groans, hooting, hissing, yelling and discordant noises'.

However, relations between employers and their workforce in the area were often good. We have seen that Francis Naish celebrated the Peace of 1801 by providing an excellent dinner to over 500 of his workpeople at Trowbridge. In 1814, Naish was once again celebrating with his workforce, this time at Twerton and following the Treaty of Paris:

> Yesterday morning, the people employed at Mr Naish's Twerton factory entered the city [of Bath] in procession – men, women and children, all dressed in holiday attire and preceded by a band of music, and displaying laurels, flags, ribbons and co. In the happy group was a car on which a loom was placed, and a man and two children cheerfully at work.

In 1828, John Stancomb entertained his workforce to celebrate the opening of his new Castle factory at Trowbridge with a grand dinner and, as we have seen, a similar occasion took place to mark the opening of a new weaving shed and the reception of William Perkins Clark junior into the firm of J and T Clarks in 1865.

Several of our family worked in the industry in times recent enough for their attitudes to be remembered. Martha Beaven (1858 – 1944), Ken's grandmother, was a power loom weaver for Brown and Palmer and had nothing but kind words, even reverence, for Sir Roger. Several of the family who worked for J. and T. Clark regarded them, as far as Ken can recollect, as employers who were on good terms with their workpeople.

How can we account for this? In the first place, until the end of the industry the factory owners lived locally, and their houses remain in profusion to remind us of this. This is known to be a contrast, for instance, to some mining districts, where the absentee mine owners invested little in the local area.

Samuel Salter, who died in 1850 with personal estates (not including his property) valued at £350,000, lived at 68, The Parade until his death. Canon Jackson, the Wiltshire historian, who knew Salter, described him as 'a civil and respectful man, who never gave himself airs'. The Norris Clarks remained at Polebarn House long after their connection to the trade ended. The Wilkins family were still manufacturing when they acquired Westcroft in 1878.

These three families lived in houses of an earlier age but most built grand houses in the nineteenth century. Along Hilperton Road there were Belfield (Thomas Clark), The Prospect (John Stancomb), Highfield (Roger Brown), The Woodlands (now called Hillbury, Arthur Perkins) and Ravenscroft (Stancombs), together with several smaller but still handsome terraces, many occupied by clothiers. In the later Victoria Road, there were Rodwell Hall (Gouldsmith), The Woodlands (MacKay) and the Laurels (Kemps). All of these have survived to the present except the Laurels.

It is almost symbolic that Springfield, almost the only Victorian mansion that no longer survives, was built by William Stancomb II (1812 – 1902) who ended his association with the trade for Farleigh House and eventually the castellated Blounts Court near Potterne.

It is worth noting that several of the clothing families of Trowbridge had roots in the town dating from the seventeenth and eighteenth centuries.

Many clothiers were philanthropic in their approach. John Waldron provided a public pump at the Town Bridge in 1830. Samuel Salter built almshouses near the Emmanuel Chapel, and the Gouldsmith family, who were also partners in Salters, provided both Trowbridge's first cottage hospital in the Halve and also a soup kitchen in Frog Lane.

Sir Roger Brown gave the Town Hall and his wife established the Lady Brown's Cottage Homes in Polebarn Road. The Clark family paid for St Thomas's Church. There also the Palmer Alms Houses in Islington. In Westbury, the Laverton Institute and the swimming baths were built by the clothing family. The Frome Literary and Scientific Institution (now Frome Museum) was given by the Simkins family of clothiers.

The major clothing families were leading lights in Trowbridge in local government, religious life and sporting life. Many of the earlier clothiers were nonconformists, like much of their workforce and the majority of cottage weavers. Thomas Clark was heavily involved in the Trowbridge Volunteers (the local Territorial force) and donated the Armoury in Brick Platt.

Reading the inscription on the front of the Market House 'Erected by William Stancomb, Lord of the Manor 1862' it might be supposed that he provided the building for the benefit of the town. In fact, he ran it as a profitable business for some years before selling it to the local authority.

Alone amongst the larger clothiers, Thomas Clark married Dorcas Pierce, a worker from his own factory – he sent her to be educated. She survived him by 39 years, living in Bellfield House until 1938 with her own deer park in the town.

TRUCK

Truck was the payment of wages to an employee by an employer by payment other than in money. Truck was by no means exclusive to this area or this industry. It was a regular source of complaint from weavers who would much rather have been paid in money, since this meant that they were not faced with the necessity of selling the goods given in lieu. In other parts of the country, factory owners paid employees partly in tokens which had to be spent in a shop controlled by the factory owner; this does not seem to have been the case locally, with the probable exception of Dunkirk Mill at Freshford where a token was issued in 1795, presumably for this purpose.

The goods paid as truck could take many forms; although truck paid to weavers was usually in the form of cloth, a whole variety of other goods included 'knives and other trifles'.

Truck was a regular source of complaint from weavers and had been forbidden by a series of Acts of Parliament, the earliest being in 1725. However, the practice continued well into the nineteenth century because of the difficulty of enforcing the legislation. This is very well illustrated by a quotation from Thomas Andrews's 'Miseries of the Miserable' of 1739.

> One day this year going into the house of a poor neighbour, a woollen manufacturer, I saw several loaves, handsome pieces of linen and woollen cloth; and taking them for signs of plenty began to congratulate the poor man upon it; ah Sir, he said, tis my misfortune to have these: I am forced to take them off my master, instead of money for my work. - I told him, it was his own fault, for the Lord lays a penalty on a master who pays in that way. To which he replied, I believe Sir you know such a poor labourer (naming him). A few years ago he was a Weaver, and refusing to be pay'd in this way, got a warrant for his master, and forced him to pay in money; when he had done so that master would let him have no more work; he went to all the masters in his way round the country, who refused him; nor has he been able to get any ever since, and must have starved, or come to the Parish, if he had not learned to work at husbandry.

Since the only way a prosecution could take place at the time was on the information (or as we would say now the statement) of the victim, they were understandably very reluctant to come forward. This is not to say that no prosecutions ever took place under the Act. Indeed, an antagonism existed between the landed gentry who were often magistrates, and the clothiers. This was despite the fact that many of the local landed gentry had their roots in clothing families; John Cooper, a justice who sentenced clothiers for the offence in 1739 had been a clothier but had given up the trade for a considerable period and instead acquired landed estates.

Even before the legislation was passed, the aristocratic James Montagu of Lackham, chairman of the Wiltshire Quarter Sessions, was critical of the clothiers and at the Easter Session of 1720, encapsulated a common view of the high-handed way in which they treated their weavers: 'Tis become a common practice, especially amongst some of those concern'd in the Woollen Manufacture, to impose Rules and Laws on the Poor they employ, and to erect Courts of Justice in every Shop and Wool-Lauft....'

Few prosecutions seem to have taken place in the eighteenth century. At a Quarter Sessions of 1739, four clothiers were convicted; however, at least two of these had their convictions overturned at a later Quarter Sessions that year.

In 1801, an advertisement appeared in the *Salisbury Journal* stating the illegality of truck and offering two guineas reward for any person giving information leading to a conviction. The advertisement was placed by a committee 'appointed by deed for putting the [Truck Acts] into execution'.

Nothing further is known of the committee but it seems to have had some effect.

An information of 1802 by Ann Barnes, widow, is not known to have led to a prosecution. Edward Culverhouse of Trowbridge, Weaver, employed her to weave a piece of cassimere. She took it home to him, for which he paid her 15/6 in money and the residue, 5/- in sundry goods. Three successful convictions in Trowbridge took place in that year and the next, two of those convicted were master weavers rather than clothiers, demonstrating that the practice was not limited to the clothiers.

In 1823, a clothier at Frome was fined £20 for the offence and in 1825 four clothiers and three master weavers at Trowbridge were also fined. That same year, the Society for Suppression of Truck was formed in Frome, and printed the petition illustrated below.

To the Gentlemen, Tradesmen, and others of the Town of Frome and its vicinity.

THE following brief outline of the points at issue between the Clothiers and their operative workmen is most humbly presented, in the full assurance that they will exert their influence and employ the talents which a merciful and gracious Providence hath entrusted to them, for the relief of their much injured and distressed neighbours. And while in common with all good subjects, we deeply deplore the evils necessarily arising from the late unhappy disturbances, and are truly and sincerely sorry that any of our fraternity should have acted in any respect contrary to the wise and necessary regulations by law established; in justice to ourselves we think it incumbent upon us, publicly and solemnly to disclaim the miserable and hacknied imputations which the interest of some, and the malice of others, have so wantonly and wickedly attributed to us. And we further beg leave to assure our fellow townsmen and his Majesty's loyal leiges in general, that we desire and aim at nothing more than we conceive to be our just due; and in order that the gentlemen and others may judge rightly of our situation, we have taken the liberty to lay before them the following state of our case. It is a well known fact, that whilst the price of our labour has been considerably reduced, the kind of work which we have been expected to perform has been rendered much worse for us, as Weavers, than it formerly was, and from hence it must be unquestionably manifest that we have for some time past been labouring under many disadvantages. Nor is this all, for in addition to the grievance above stated, we have been exposed to the most cruel and unprincipled imposition which the Truckstering spirit of the age could possibly devise. Woollen Cloth and Linen Drapery articles, of very inferior quality, have been forced upon us at an excessive and unreasonable price; Knives, Spoons, Tickets, Stone Blue, &c. have been tendered to us as an equivalent for our labour. To complain was useless, and to inform against our employers had been our destruction; as too many of the Master Manufacturers have in some way or other given in to this iniquitous practice. To remedy these evils, and to obtain redress, is the sole object which we have in view, and we appeal to the justice,

In November 1825, the *Devizes Gazette* reported that 'several clothiers and weavers were convicted at Trowbridge about two months since of paying their workmen in goods instead of money. Which one of the parties convicted, having discovered that the principal informer (Robert Reeves) was at the time pursuing the same practice, four informations were lodged against him, and he was on Tuesday convicted on one of them in the penalty of £20; the other three were adjourned.'

Nevertheless, the truck system persisted. In February 1829, the *Devizes Gazette* reported that 'the poor workmen are dreadfully oppressed by the bad system among the small manufacturers of paying in truck'. Later that year, the Trowbridge Union (which we shall discuss later) had printed the words of a song or poem which included:

> Here we our varied griefs impart;
> We join in hand and join in heart:
> Against truck trade we all unite,
> For none can call such practice right
>
> Truck trade we ever shall deplore,
> That vile oppression of the poor
> The humbug clothiers in our day
> Do with vile trash their workmen pay.
>
> There fine truck clothiers keep a store
> Of trash to cheat and grind the poor;
> And charge for bacon, soap or cheese
> Double the price where'r they please
>
> But this is not, we know full well,
> One half the goods that these men sell;
> They've humbugs laces, knives, and tape,
> Bak'd apples, butter bread and crape.

In 1831, a further Truck Act was passed which increased fines for offenders, made any contract where payment was partly by truck null and void, and entitled the person who was paid in truck to keep the truck payment and claim his or her full wages.

In his 1840 Report, Austin said that some smaller capitalists, in their struggle against the improved machinery of the extensive manufacturers, resort to low wages and truck. This seems to be confirmed by the *Devizes Gazette* report above. We find it hard to believe that major clothiers like Salters and Clarks resorted to such a practice. It is likely to have been limited to the smaller clothiers and less scrupulous master weavers.

Although there were small clothiers until the 1870s, no more is heard of truck either in newspaper reports or in the reminiscences of weavers. It may be that the practice was generally frowned on and gradually died out.

An amusing anecdote was that the partners in the firm of Palmer and Mackay used to say that the little shop building at the end of Ashton Street used to be a truck shop. In fact, it was not built until 1873, surely far too late for such a purpose. However, the poem by the Trowbridge Union would seem to imply that workers were limited to purchase of inferior goods, which may suggest that they could only use certain shops, possibly kept by relatives of friends of the employer.

THE CONSERVATIVE WEAVER

WE HAVE ALREADY noted the distrust of cottage weavers towards new technology, especially towards the use of spring looms. An attempt to introduce them in Trowbridge in 1792 resulted in riotous opposition and failure. Spring looms were gradually introduced in shop weaving but not without continued opposition from the cottage weavers.

In 1816 the *Bath Chronicle* reported the following:-

> Tuesday morning the magistrates of Bradford having received information that the weavers were coming there in the course of the day to break the spring looms, etc. the gentlemen and all the principal housekeepers were sworn in special constables, being determined to resist such illegal proceedings; and between 3 and 4 o'clock accounts were brought in that a very large number, several hundreds, were advancing and within a mile of the town, and had begun to break some looms to pieces in the houses on the road. The magistrates and constables immediately proceeded to the spot, when (the Riot Act being read) they took into custody such of the rioters, about thirty, as were pointed out to have been concerned in the mischief, which was done, and eventually dispersed the rest of the mob. Upon examination of the prisoners before the magistrates, eight who were identified and sworn to as being the most active, were committed and sent off to Devizes Bridewell, to take their trials at Salisbury Assizes; eight more were remanded for further examination the next morning and the rest were suffered to depart home, having entered into recognizances to keep the peace for twelve months and to appear to answer the charge when called upon.

An even larger such event took place in 1822 beginning at Dilton Marsh when a body of 1100 or 1200 attacked spring looms at Warminster, Corsley, Crockerton and Heytesbury.

> On Saturday sennight the weavers again assembled at Dilton Marsh and forcibly [took] from looms in an unfinished state three pieces of broad cloth belonging to a manufacturer at Warminster. They then, in a body of 1100 or 1200, marched to that town, taking with them the pieces on the beams of the looms, with a view to intimidate the manufacturer there into a compliance with their demands, but finding the clothiers firm in their resolution to withstand any alteration in prices, they proceeded to the homes of the different weavers in the town and neighbourhood and breaking open the weaving shops, took the pieces from the looms and brought them home to the respective owners. Towards the evening they assembled in a large body before the house of one of the manufacturers in Warminster, bursting open the gates and damaging the windows etc. of the dwelling house. The constables to the number of about twenty attended being the force that could then be assembled but were of course incompetent to disperse such a body. The rioters, however, finding the manufacturers continued firm, at length dispersed. Early on Monday morning the neighbouring Magistrates assembled, and before the middle of the day the Warminster Troop of Yeomanry, commanded by W. Long, esq: mustered and marched into the town. The weavers however had changed the scene of their operations, and avoiding Warminster, proceeded in large bodies through Corsley, Crockerton and to Heytesbury; at all which places, finding the manufacturers fully resolved to withstand any alteration in prices, they demolished the spring looms (more than fifty in all) and took off the pieces in an unfinished state...

From this date nothing further is found about violence against spring looms but it is quite possible that they were never used in cottage weaving.

Spring looms were not the only innovation which was opposed by cottage weavers. The was violent opposition to an improvement to handlooms invented by Isaac Wheeler of Dilton Marsh in 1796.

The Quarter Sessions Great Roll for Hilary 1796 relates as follows.

> On 4 November 1795 Joseph Baily, Thomas Lanfear, and James Lanfear the younger, all of Dilton Marsh, weavers, came to the house of Isaac Wheeler there and forcibly took him to the house of Stephen Smith, another weaver there, where they made him destroy a small wheel which he had made and put on Smith's broad loom. They then made him destroy a wheel which he had put

on Jeremiah Millard's loom. They then took Wheeler to his own house, where James Lanfear wanted to break it open, but it was not done. Instead, they carried him round the common at Dilton Marsh, then to Leigh and Westbury, and brought him back to Westbury Town's end, and from whence they pelted him with potatoes and dirt until he came to the brook opposite Mrs. Phipps at Westbury Leigh. They threw him into the brook, and kept him there for some considerable time. Finally they drove him down the street to Pipins bridge, where the two Lanfears and John Lanfear threw him into the water again and kept him for some time with his head under water till he was nearly suffocated.

There can be little doubt that the wheels made by Wheeler were intended to take up the cloth as it was woven. His device therefore pre-dates by some years the one mentioned in Rees's *Cyclopaedia*, as patented by Mr. James Hall in 1803, or the one known to Miss Mann in the *History of Technology* patented in the name of Thomas Johnson in 1805. Both used a ratchet wheel at the end of the cloth beam which was wound round by a catch fitted to the slay. Although we cannot be sure that turning on mechanisms were ever fitted to cottage looms in our area, the innovation would surely have been to the weavers' advantage as it would have speeded up the process.

Similarly, we have seen from James Allen's memoirs that cottage weavers performed extraordinarily complex work using seven treadles despite the fact that pre-selector devices already available such as the witch and dobbie would have limited the number of treadles to two.

Anthony Austin noted of the weavers of Gloucestershire 1840: 'Weavers are jealous of any alteration and unwilling to be put out of their way'. This also appears to be true of the cottage weavers in our area.

THE RADICAL WEAVER

IT IS HARD to imagine now how volatile our area was in the eighteenth and early nineteenth centuries, with frequent rioting and the resultant dispatch of troops. We have seen how hard the lives of the weavers could be, subject as they were to depression in trade over which they had no control, but we have also seen how a deep resistance to change could lead to violent disorder.

A bad harvest in 1726 sent up the price of bread, and this was coupled with a financial crisis following the declaration of war with Spain. This and the subsequent shortage of cash and stagnation of trade led, for instance, the Trowbridge clothiers Usher and Jefferies to decide to send no more cloth to London until there was some prospect of it being sold.

The weavers also complained of a heavy fall in wage rates, and particularly of two grievances which were of long standing; these were the use of weights containing 17 ounces to the pound and the lengthening of the warps by 3 or 4 yards.

At Bradford on 23rd November 'the weavers there rose in great numbers and broke by force into the house of several clothiers, put some of 'em in danger of their lives by stoning their houses &c, and forced them to promise them what they demanded'. Other incidents took place at Melksham and between Trowbridge and Devizes. When the High Sheriff of Wiltshire arrived with a force of dragoons he was knocked to the ground.

Nevertheless the authorities were conciliatory and let it be known that grievances would be redressed if peaceful application were made. Representatives of both sides were subsequently summoned to appear before the Privy Council. Articles of agreement were drawn up which provided for the use of proper weights and warping bars of fixed length, and these were immediately embodied in an Act of Parliament. This led to a permanent change from payment by the piece to payment by the yard.

There were further riots in 1738. Henry Colthurst, a clothier at Melksham, was applied to by a weaver from near Trowbridge for a chain. This weaver was 'not only poor but destitute of work', and was given a chain to weave at 14d a yard, which was the price given by Colthurst and all other Melksham clothiers for many years past.

If this was strictly true, it is hard to see what provoked the riot. However, it seems clear that weavers from the Trowbridge area believed, rightly or wrongly, that Colthurst was paying a low rate, and was also guilty of paying in truck. They told the weaver that they would cut his chain unless he could get Colthurst to increase his rate by 1d a yard, and he went to Melksham to inform Colthurst of this. Before he could return (whether with an increased offer or not we do not know), a mob of weavers was formed, which cut the chains in looms about Trowbridge, Studley, and Hilperton, and then set out for Melksham.

On their way they were met by two successive messengers from Colthurst to say that he would pay 1d a yard more. The weavers required a Note of Hand to ensure this, which one of the messengers gave them. According to the Melksham clothiers, however, the mob was now bent on plunder. They entered the town, and on their way to Colthurst's house (on the site of the offices of the Avon Rubber Co.) cut three chains which belonged to other clothiers in one weaving shop.

Colthurst had left the town by this time, and the weavers broke into his house, destroyed his furniture, drank his beer and wine, and threw his wool, yarn, and implements into the river. They then returned to the Market Place, where they demanded and were given a note, signed by all the clothiers in the town that they would give 15d a yard for weaving and 1s for spooling from then on.

Most then returned home, but 'two desperate and leading villains' had seen some finished cloths in the passing shop, which had escaped the earlier attack. They went back about 7 o' clock, but were opposed by some neighbours who had gone back to the house to guard what was left of Colthurst's goods. These caught one man, John Crabb, but the other jumped out of a high window and went off to tell the weavers of Crabb's capture.

Early next morning Crabb was taken before the Justices at Chippenham and committed to gaol at Salisbury. In the meantime, a much greater mob, said to number 1,500, was marching towards Melksham. They sent messengers ahead saying that unless the Melksham clothiers prevented the committal of Crabb, they would demolish the rest of Colthurst's houses. The clothiers wrote to the Justices asking that Crabb might not be committed, and sent a copy of the letter to the mob, who were still outside the town.

This did not appease them, and they continued into the town, completed the destruction of Colthurst's house, and threw so much of his household and clothing goods into the river that the river was strewn with them for miles. When the messenger to the Justices returned without Crabb they destroyed his shear shop and the cloths in it. They then attacked some houses belonging to Colthurst, destroying one. Then they destroyed other houses in the town and the grist and fulling mills.

The next day they continued destroying the ruins of Colthurst's premises. Parties of them were posted to intercept Crabb on his way to prison, but he was sent round through Marlborough. They said they would not leave the town until they had Crabb, and that they would level the town unless he was brought to them in the Market Place. However, food and drink were running out, and eventually they obliged the clothiers to enter into a bond of £10,000 to produce Crabb in ten days' time.

Even then they continued destruction at Colthurst's. In the afternoon the Justices read the Riot Act. On this, some dispersed, but others continued their destruction until night. They then left the town. The next Monday they threatened another incursion, but by then there were troops in the town, and so they desisted.

Crabb and two others involved in the riots were tried at Salisbury Assizes, found guilty and hanged. Nine more were imprisoned and one was acquitted. Unlike the 1726 riots, those of 1738 had little positive effect on the lives of the weavers. The incident gave rise to a lengthy correspondence in the newspapers and pamphlets, including *The Case as it Now Stands* and *Miseries of the Miserable*, referred to above, and also through various publications by both the clothiers and the weavers themselves. Truck remained an important bone of contention, but is not clear whether the Melksham clothiers honoured their promise of 15d a yard.

In 1750, troops were sent to west Wiltshire 'in order to curb and put a stop to the riotous Proceedings of the Weavers and other Manufacturers, who, from the great Wages lately given are grown idle and debauched, and which, if not put a stop to, will occasion most of the principal Manufacturers [here meaning employers] to lay down trade .... And thereby many Thousand Poor being unemployed. We strongly suggest that William Temple sent this to the newspaper.

Further riots occurred in 1766 as a result of high bread prices and North Bradley mill was burnt down; these riots were not specifically related to any cause of the weavers but it would be surprising if no weavers were involved.

We have already discussed the riots of 1787 and 1792 against shop weaving and the use of spring looms. Dragoons were quartered at Trowbridge and Bradford in consequence. In 1795 there was yet another riot in Trowbridge, this time about the price of food.

The events of 1803 which culminated in the destruction of Littleton Mill at Seend and the execution of Thomas Hilliker were about the introduction of finishing machinery and therefore did not directly affect weavers, but given the febrile atmosphere of the period locally, it is quite possible that some weavers took part.

As well as the protests against spring looms at Warminster and surrounding places in 1822 referred to above, there were other riots that year. In January there were protests in Bradford, Trowbridge and Frome where a number of spring looms were broken or stripped of their cloths before the Riot Act was read and the Yeomanry deployed.

In 1826 there were further food riots in Bradford and Trowbridge concerning the artificial inflation of the price of potatoes by a local market gardener. The *Devizes Gazette* contrasted the local area with Lancashire, where there had also been riots: 'At Trowbridge, on the other hand, although considerable distress may, and certainly does exist ... the outrages must be attributed, in great measure, to mere wantonness'. Once again, the Yeomanry marched into the towns amidst 'the hooting and the hissing of the mob'.

There had been societies of weavers from the eighteenth century locally, such as Loyal Society of Broad-Cloth Weavers, which was in existence by 1733, but these would have been more of the nature of a friendly society than a trade union. We have already seen that the weavers were capable of coming together for a common cause against trade practices or employers, sometimes trying to obtain legal guarantees from the clothiers.

The struggles of the shearmen against mechanisation had led to industrial organisation as early as 1788 when journeymen clothworkers in Bradford were prosecuted for conspiring to prevent innovations, and by 1803 an established trade union had been formed in Trowbridge, issuing a printed membership card.

In 1824, the Combination Acts preventing labour organisations were repealed. The following year the Society for Suppression of Truck was active in Frome, issuing a printed manifesto.

By 1829, the Westbury weavers at Matravers and Overbury struck for wages, which was possibly because the firm employed them in a weaving shop. A Union was formed in Trowbridge to support the Westbury strikers, and according to the much later reminiscences of John Foley, the parish constable of Trowbridge at the time, £200 were sent to them each week, an enormous sum. The Union was certainly in evidence in Trowbridge – writing in his diary the young W. H. Tucker said 'about this time the ill-fated 'union' was in all its glory and a great proportion of the operatives of this district entered it. It was liberally patronized by the trade's people and the middling classes – prayer meetings were held on its behalf and the principal members walked in solemn procession, headed by one of their number appareled in the robes of a bishop. Overbury's workpeople had lately turned out for wages, and came over from Westbury weekly to the Blue Bowl, where they received their allowance, and as the window of our counting house faced that respectable inn, we had a good opportunity of studying their physiognomy'.

The strike coincided with a trade depression of unprecedented hardship. In Frome, 5,000 people were said to be unemployed. The government took the unusual step of sending an inspector to the district to report and said of Trowbridge that he had never encountered 'such a scene of rags and ghastly faces' as in the queue to receive parish relief.

According to Foley, the Union foundered when the treasurer absconded to America with the remaining funds. The demise of the Union did not mark the end of an organised workforce in the district. Nationally, demands for more political representation, better industrial relations and the abolition of unfair trade practices coalesced into the Chartist movement. Trowbridge became a notable centre of Chartist activity, as has been extensively covered by M.J. Lansdown in his *The Trowbridge Chartists 1838 – 1848*.

Whilst we will not recite the entire history of Chartism locally, it is worth mentioning the involvement of weavers in the movement and add to Michael Lansdown's research. In 1840 Jacob Hawkins, a baker, acquired premises in Shails Lane. The purchase was followed by a trust deed establishing a Chartist Democratic Chapel. Of the thirteen trustees, two were weavers – Henry Salisbury and Charles Hill.

The Democratic Chapel was later the Harp Inn and photographed shortly before demolition in the 1960s.

These and others had united in forming a Working Mens' Association Trust to hold the premises to be 'used by the Society to meet for the purpose of carrying on therein the worship of the only living and true God in accordance with the forms, doctrines, and discipline of Protestant Dissenters, and also for promoting the instruction and edification of the young and rising generation, the advancement and improvement of political intellect among the labouring classes, and the diffusion of scientific and general knowledge among society at large conformably with the laws and statutes of this realm'. Prior to relocating to Shails Lane the Association had rented part of Trowbridge Barracks until it was repurchased by the government in 1839.

In 1840 and 1841 the Democratic Chapel was mortgaged to Enoch Stanton, a weaver of Sandridge Hill near Melksham. In each deed it was described as lately converted into a chapel and various rooms and into two houses. In 1844 Stanton had taken possession, and the premises were put up for sale. They consisted of a meeting house and committee and council rooms called the Democratic Chapel, a house called the Charter House with grocer's shop, and another house.

The principal local Chartists, William Potts, a Trowbridge druggist, and William Carrier, clothworker, were arrested and imprisoned in 1839. Doubtless many weavers were involved in the local Chartist movement – they are occasionally mentioned in the newspapers, for example in March 1839 when 'about 150 weavers and others, with a band of music and with some flags with incendiary inscriptions' entered Devizes.

With Carrier and Potts in prison, Chartism in the district continued as a more peaceable movement of social activity, discussion, education and propaganda.

From the mid-1840s the local industry entered a period of prosperity which as we have seen enabled many handweavers to go on obtaining work until the mid-1870s. As we have discussed, some strikes took place during this period but there were no more riots connected with the industry.

CONCLUSION

THE TEXTILE INDUSTRY of west Wiltshire is long gone but the mark it has made on the landscape of the area remains today. The last factory closed in 1982 but the area is a treasure house of buildings connected with the industry, not only the factories and workshops but also the homes of the handloom and factory weavers.

INDEX

This is an index primarily of people and places, but includes also a few technical terms. Streets and minor names are in Trowbridge unless stated otherwise. Other places are mostly in Wiltshire or neighbouring areas of Somerset.

abb 3, 126–7, 129
Abbey Mill, Bradford 85, 116, 118
Abbott, John 87
Adcroft 11
Adlam, Samuel 51
Aldridge, Richard 127
Allen, James 48, 103, 173
Alma Street 149
alms 167
almshouses 23, 166, 167
America 151, 177
Andrews, Thomas 153, 168
Angel Mill, Westbury 117
Angolas 103
Anstie, John 84–5, 89–90, 95–6
Appleby, Samuel 11
Arnold (weaver) 75
Assizes, Salisbury 171, 175
Austin, Anthony 100, 102, 107, 122, 153, 155, 170, 173
automatics 125
Avon, River (Bristol) 1,
Avon Rubber 118, 174
Axe and Cleaver, North Bradley 40, 79

back–to–back housing 53, 71
Bailey, Edward 137
Bailey (Baily), Joseph 95, 172
Bailey, Joshua 154
Bailey's Shop 147
Baines, Edward 99, 100
Barnes, Ann 169
Barracks, Trowbridge 179
Barratt, James 127
Batchelor, John 48
Bath 83, 89, 165
Batheaston factory 97
Beavan, William 148
Beaven, James 1

Beaven, Martha 166
Beckington 147
Belcombe Brook 87
Bellfield House 166–7
Berrett, Roy 91
Bethesda Church 58
Bettey, Joe 35
Biggs, Jesse 133
Biss 30–1
Biss, River 12, 16
Biss Wood 29
Bitton Mill, Westbury 117
Black Ball 29–31
Black Horse Inn 25
Black Swan Inn 161
Blackwell Hall 91
Blanchard, Walter 163
Blounts Court, Potterne 166
Bodman, James 20, 74
Boutcher, Benjamin 11
Boyers (Bowyer's) Mill, Westbury Leigh 98, 116, 165
Bradford on Avon 6, 12, 16, 18, 38, 41, 43, 81–3, 87, 91, 95–7, 103, 116–18, 122, 125, 127, 130, 133, 149, 151, 155, 159–60, 163, 165, 171, 174, 176–7
Bradford Road 68
Bradley, North 16, 20, 23, 29, 31–2, 37, 39–40, 79, 87, 96, 120, 122–3, 130, 142–3, 147, 151, 159–62, 164, 176
Bradley Common 80
Bradley Road 23–4
Bratton 37, 121, 153
Bray, William 132–4, 137
Bricker, James 163
Bridge (Brig, Burds, Burge) Gate 10–11
Bridge House 146
Bridge Mill 92, 97, 111–12, 125

Brokerswood 29, 31, 79
Bromham 89, 154
Brooke, Thomas 101
Broughton Gifford 105, 123, 157
Brown, Lady 167
Brown, Sir Roger 71, 133, 146, 167
Brown, Samuel 71
Brown, William 71
Brown and Palmer 75, 107, 111, 122–3, 132–3, 139, 145–6, 150, 165–6
Bulkington 100, 163
Bull, John 17
Bull, William 38
Burds (Bridge, Brig, Burge) Gate 10–11
Burges, Henry 37
Burges, John 37
Butcher, Joseph 159
Butcher, Robert 159
Bythesea Road 64

Cadby's Yard 7
Callaway, Roger 37
Calne 81, 100, 126
Canal Road 57
Carr's of Twerton 103
Castle Court Mill, 107, 113
Castle Factory, 102, 166
Castle Street 7, 41, 58–62, 147–8
Chapman, Thomas 149
Chapmanslade 38, 97–8
Charfield Mill (Glos) 132
Charter House 179
Chartism, Chartists 177–9
Chartist Democratic Chapel 178
Chartist's Square 12
Cherry Gardens 74
Chippenham 37, 81, 83, 85, 88–9, 96, 117, 119, 127, 149, 151, 175
Chittoe 129
Clark, John 83, 91, 107
Clark, Thomas 108, 167
Clark, William Perkins 149, 166
Clark, Messrs J and T, 103, 107–9, 117, 125, 132–3, 137–40, 143, 149, 166, 170
Clift, Sarah 130, 132
Cobbett, William 151
Cobourg Place 53
Cockall, J and J 98
Cogswell, Benjamin 92
Cogswell, Edwin 121

Cogswell, James 87, 103, 121, 123, 154
Coldharbour 30
Coles, James 83, 147
College Road 23
Colthurst, Henry 174–5
Conigre 9, 42, 75–8, 93, 133
Cook, John 83, 91
Cook, Samuel 84, 86
Cook and Naish 96
Coombs, Edward 56
Coombs, Thomas, 160
Cooper, Benjamin 97, 107
Cooper, John 168
Corsham 126
Corsley 172
Cottle's Barton 7
Court Hill 95
Court Street 58, 61–2
Cox, Edward 14
Crabb, John 175
Cradle Bridge 123, 149
Cradle Bridge Mill 113, 125
Crockerton 172
Croft, The 24
Cross, Nicholas and John 83, 91
Cross Street 53
Crump, W B 101
Cuckoo's Corner 24, 133
Culverhouse, Edward 169
Cuzner, Bladud 130

Dalton 101
Daniels, — 150
Davis, James 78
Deane, Mr 91
Defoe, Daniel 82
Delamere Road 55
Democratic Chapel 178–9
Deverall, Robert 48
Deverall, William 65, 149
Devizes 84–5, 89–90, 95–6, 99, 126–7, 129, 171, 174, 179
Dicks, John 75
Dilton Marsh 34–5, 123, 137–9, 140–1, 146, 150, 153–4, 160, 163, 172–3
Dobcross type looms 108, 125
Dodsmead Corner 29
Doell, Richard 128
Dorrington, Michael 164
Dorset 35

Downhayes 15
Drynham 19, 22
Drynham Farm 16
Drynham Road 18, 20
Duke Street 7, 9, 43, 78, 86, 91, 108
Duke Street Mill 113, 132
Dunford families 22
Dunkirk 167
Dunn 133
Dursley 18–19, 22, 71, 78, 146, 160
Dymott 40, 81

East Field 10–11
Edmonds, Mr 165
Edmonds, Moore and, 120, 123, 125
Edwards, Joseph 11
Elderton, James 82
Emmanuel Chapel 166
Esgair Moel Woollen Mill 5

Farleigh Castle 9
Farleigh House 166
Farleigh Hungerford 120, 123, 125, 133
Fisher, P H 128
Fisherton Anger 127
Foley, John 177
Fore Street 7–9
Foyle, Samuel 137
Francis, James 154
Frawley, Robert 149
Freshford 96, 130, 167
Freshford Mill 97, 117, 120, 123, 125, 150
Frog Lane 76, 133, 167
Frome 1, 35, 81, 83, 85, 89, 96, 99–100, 109, 113, 117, 119–20, 130, 132, 161, 169, 176–7
Frome Literary and Scientific Institution 167
Frome Road 18, 23, 25
Frome Society for Prosecuting Felons 127

Gingell, William 154
Glastonbury 94
Gloucester Road 14, 17, 67
Gloucestershire 96–7, 102–3, 129, 132, 143, 173
Gouldsmith family 166
Graham, John Long 150
Graham, Robert 150
Green Lane, Southwick 39–40
Greenland Mill, Bradford 97, 117–18

Haines, John 130
Haley of Frome 109, 112–13, 115–17
Halifax 2
Hall, James 173
Halve, The 9–10, 41, 167
Hancock, Sarah 11
Hanson and Mills 91–2
Harding, William 128
Harford, Richard 20
Harford, William 20
Harp Inn 178
Harper, Simon 132–3
Harris, James 131
Harris, Superintendent 133
Harrop, Joseph 116, 165
Harvett (Harford) 20
Hawkins, Jacob 178
Haycock, Lorna 90–1
Hayward, J and E 13, 103, 115
Hayward, John 149
Heath, Ralph 93
Henbest's Barton 8
Hewitt and Kemp 103
Heytesbury 107, 151, 172
Highfield 166
Hill, Charles 178
Hill, Francis 95–6
Hill, I 161
Hill Gate 12
Hill Street 70, 92
Hillbury 166
Hillier, George 130–1
Hilliker, Thomas 93, 176
Hillman, Ogden and 83
Hilperton 7, 14, 38, 40, 81, 154, 160, 174
Hilperton Lane 11–12
Hilperton Marsh 27, 39, 80, 34, 127, 154
Hilperton Road 10, 14, 75, 166
Holbrook Farm 16
Holbrook Lane 18–20
Holland, James 142
Holloway, Job 11
Holt 117
Holwell, William 48
Hooper, John 98
Hoopers Pool 39, 80
Horningsham 92
Houlton, Joseph 11
Houlton family 9

Huddersfield 99, 101
Hungerford crest 9
Hungerford, Farleigh 120, 123, 125, 133

Innox Mill 114–15
Innoxes, The 14
Ireland (in North Bradley) 31, 39, 79
Islay (Scotland) 37
Islington (Trowbridge) 15–16, 53–8, 167
Islington Gardens 53

Jackson, Canon John E 9, 166
Janes, Joseph 123, 133
Jefferies, Usher and 173
Jenkins, David 102
Jenkins, J G 102
Jesser, William 83, 85
Johnson, Thomas 173
Jones, John 96–7, 122, 130
Jones, Hart, Jones and Co 147
Joyce, Cooper and Co 97
Joyce, Thomas 96

Kemp, E and J 103
Kemp family 166
Kingsbridge (Southwick) 79
King's Arms 28

Lackham 168
Lacock 160
Ladd, Henry 37
Ladydown Mill 12
Lambert's Marsh 29
Lancashire 176
Lanfear, Benjamin 137, 172
Lanfear, James 137, 172–3
Lanfear, John 173
Lanfear, Thomas 172–3
Lansdown, Michael J 177, 178
Laurels, The 166
Laverton family 117
Laverton Institute 167
Leach and Sons 108, 117
Leeds 99–100
Lewis, Daniel 140, 146
Lintern, John 78
Littleton Mill 93, 176
Lloyd, Daniel 96
London 15, 82, 92, 103, 173
Long, Charles 76–7

Long, Nathaniel 38
Long, Robert 147
Long, Thomas 7
Long, William 130
Long and Co 132
Long family (Rood Ashton) 31
Longfield House 63
Longleat 98
Lucas, Daniel 71, 137–9, 143, 145, 147, 149
Lucas, William 130

Mackay family 166
Mackay, Palmer and 4, 84, 108, 171
Maddox, John 149
Malmesbury 95–6
Malmesbury Abbey 85
Mann, Julia de Lacy 96, 102, 107, 173
Mannings, Matthew 10
Market House 8, 167
Market Place 175
Marlborough 175
Marler, John 11
Marsh, Thomas 128
Marshman, Ann 160
Marshman, John 38
Marshman's Yard 8
Martyn family 31
Matravers and Co 111, 117
Matravers and Overbury 165, 177
Matthews, Cornelius 163
Mattock, William 137
Melksham 81, 83, 87–9, 91, 100, 111, 117–18, 125–6, 129–30, 147, 151, 163, 174–6, 179
Mere 92, 164
Miles, Nathaniel 154
Miles, William A 143
Millard, Jeremiah 173
Millard of Trowbridge 109, 112–13, 116–17
Mills, Hanson and 91–2
Mitchell, Eliza 133
Montagu, James 3, 168
Moon, George 126
Moor, James 159
Moore and Edmonds 120, 123, 125
Moore, Mr 133
Morris, Mr 121, 123
Mortimer, Edward Horlock 83, 146
Mortimer, John 149
Mortimer Street 44, 63–5, 71, 130, 149

Naish, Francis 78, 92–3, 99, 165
Naish, Cook and 96
Naish's Yard 70
Nemnich, Philipp Andreas 97
Newtown (Trowbridge) 14, 18, 41, 43, 65–6, 68, 75, 121
Niblett, John 147
Noad, Mr 143
Nomansland 36
Norris, Frederick 150
Norris Clark family 166
North Bradley 16, 20, 23, 29, 31–2, 37, 39–40, 79, 87, 96, 120, 122–23, 130, 142–3, 147, 151, 159–62, 164, 176
Northgate Street (Devizes) 95

Ogden and Hillman 83
Overbury, Matravers and 165, 177
Oxford 126

Palmer Alms Houses 167
Palmer and Mackay 4, 84, 108, 171
Palmer, Brown and 75, 107, 111, 122–3, 132–3, 139, 145–6, 150, 165–6

Palmer Gardens 14, 54–5,
Parade, The 166
Paris Exhibition 103
Park Street 23
Parsons Corner 79
Parsons, Isaac 137, 140, 144, 146
Paxcroft 30
Perkins, Benjamin 149
Perkins, James 147–8
Phelps, William 91
Phipps, Mrs 173
Pierce, Dorcas 167
Pike, Thomas 122
Pipins Bridge 173
Pitt, Fred 12
Plat(t), The Brick 12, 71–2, 167
Platt (loom maker) 109
Plunketts, Hanson and Mills 91
Polebarn Buildings 70
Polebarn House 166
Polebarn Road 71, 167
Poleshole (Southwick) 79
Ponting, Kenneth 102
Porter, John 7

Porter's Barton 7
Potterne 166
Potts, William 179
Pourch, Edward 11, 13
Purnell, David 128

Rackfield Place (Twerton) 93–4
Radstock 36, 151
Randall, Stephen 137–40, 143–6, 150
Rank, The (North Bradley) 40, 79
Ravenscroft 166
Read, William 123
Read's Yard 9
Reeves, Robert 170
Regent Place (Bradford) 81
Reynolds, Esau 74
Richmond, Thomas 73–4, 129
Riverway 12
Robbins, Jacob 129
Rode 31, 79–80, 89, 95, 143, 147
Rode Common 38, 80
Rode Hill 31
Rodney House 86
Rodway (Rodaway) James 132–4, 137
Rodwell Hall 166
Rose and Crown 14
Roundstone Street 7–8
Russia 90–91
Rutland Crescent 19
Rutter, Daniel 63

St Stephen's Place 58, 63
Salisbury 36, 83, 93, 127, 153, 175
Salisbury Assizes 171
Salisbury, Henry 178
Salisbury Plain 153
Salter, Samuel (and Co) 1, 84, 91, 103, 113, 115, 125, 142, 149, 166, 167, 170
Sanderson 89
Sandridge Hill (Melksham) 179
Sargent, Joseph 160
Sartain, Robert 163
Saunders, Joseph 129
Schofield (loom maker) 108–9, 112, 116
Scotland, Scottish 31, 37, 124
Scott, Joseph 130
Scutts Bridge 123
Seend 37, 81, 176
Selfe, James 83, 86, 146
Selwood Iron Works (Frome) 117

Semington 29
Seymour Estate 11
Shails Lane 12, 76, 178–9
Sheppard, Edward 97, 130, 131, 142
Sheppard, Walter 83
Sheppard, William 83, 85, 96
Shires, The 1, 7, 14
Shrubbs (Freshford) 130
Sidnell, George 132
Silverthorne family 29, 31
Silverthorne's Court 7–8
Silverthorne, John 29
Simkins family 167
Simms, Robert 163
Sims, James 78
Singer, Richard 83, 85, 96, 161
Singer, — 161
Slade, Henry 137–8, 144, 146
Slocombe, Ivor 38
Smith, Stephen 172
Smith, W and Brothers 108
Snailum, George 39
Southwick 29, 31, 33, 39–40, 79–80
Springfield 166
Stainer's Buildings 58, 61
Stallard Street 14, 17, 75, 146
Stallard, John 17
Stancomb, Arthur Perkins 75, 166
Stancomb, John (and Sons) 102–3, 125, 134, 166
Stancomb, William 142, 147, 167
Stancomb, W and J 149
Stanton, Enoch 179
Staverton 14, 27, 78–9, 96–7, 107, 117, 122, 130, 147, 154
Stevens, John 159
Stillman, John and Thomas 83
Stoney Littleton 97
Stowford Mill 130
Stratton, Jospeh 121
Stroud 1, 102, 128, 147
Studley 1, 16, 18, 20–1, 23–6, 37–8, 78, 159, 161, 174
Studley Fields 74, 78
Studley Mill 14, 108, 110
Stump, William 85

Tadd, Avril 36
Taunton 98
Temple, William 152, 154, 158–9, 176

Thatcher, Inspector 132
Timbrell Cottages 23
Timbrell Street 15, 44–8, 50, 53, 56, 58, 78, 130–1
Timbrell family 15
Timbrell, Thomas 21, 23
Toop, William 137
Trapnell, William 45, 48
Trowle Common 159
Trowle Lane 18, 68
Tucker, Samuel 147
Tucker, W H 177
Turleigh 38
Twerton 1, 78, 93–4, 99, 103, 107, 165

Uley 96–7, 130
Union Street 11, 71, 123
Upton Lovell 107
Usher, Henry 146, 173

Vallis Way Mill (Frome) 117, 120
Victoria Mill 120, 123
Victoria Street 166
Vince, — 163

Waite, Shaphan 160–1
Walbridge Mill (Frome) 117, 119
Waldon, John 86
Waldron, John 166
Walker, George 146
Walker, Joseph 131–2
Walker, Peter 95
Walker, William 144–5, 150
Walker's 132, 144
Wansey, Henry 83
Warminster 81, 151, 172, 176
Waterford Mill (Chippenham) 117, 119
Waylen, Robert 95, 99
Webb, John Henry (and Co) 86, 103, 111–12, 125, 130, 132, 142
Weeke (Wyke) Marsh 27
Welsh Folk Museum 5
Wesley Road 68
West Ashton 29, 31
Westbury 1, 81, 92–3, 98, 100, 116–17, 147, 150, 153–4, 160, 163, 165, 167, 173, 177
Westcroft 86, 166
Wheeler, Isaac 172–3
White Hart inn 158

White Trough 26
Whiterow 26, 39, 78, 142
Wicker Hill 92
Wicks, James 120, 123, 133
Wicks, William 149
Wilkins, William (and Co) 107, 133
Wilkins family 166
Wilkinson, Revd John 105, 109, 123, 157
Willis, Anne 37
Willis, George 154
Wilshire, John 91
Wilson, John 160
Wilton 160, 163
Wingfield 16, 160

Woodmarsh 39, 79
Woodward, John 150
Worcester 126
Wotton-under-Edge 132
Wyke Marsh 27

Yarnbrook 29, 31, 79
Yarnbrook Road 32
Yerbury Street 41, 69, 78, 116, 149
Yerbury, Francis 82–4, 87
York Buildings 54
York Place 48
Yorkshire 1, 12, 91, 99–101, 105, 112

www.ingramcontent.com/pod-product-compliance
Lightning Source LLC
Chambersburg PA
CBHW042138160426
43200CB00020B/2972